THE
ZULU WAR

THE
ZULU WAR
ISANDHLWANA TO ULUNDI

MICHAEL BARTHORP

CASSELL&CO

Cassell & Co
Wellington House, 125 Strand
London WC2R 0BB

First published in 1980
This edition 2002

British Library Cataloguing-in-Publication data:
A catalogue record for this book is available from the British Library

ISBN 0-304-36270-0

Printed and bound in Slovenia by Mladinska knjiga tiskarna d.d.,
Ljubljana by arrougement
With Prešernova družba d.d.

Contents

To my wife,
who walked the fields of
Isandhlwana, Rorke's Drift
and
Ulundi

Foreword

Although a century has passed since the Zulu War of 1879, its dramatic events and the courage displayed by men of both sides have continued to exercise a peculiar fascination which has not been eclipsed by the much greater conflicts that have occurred since. By modern standards, and indeed to many Victorians, the British invasion of the independent kingdom of Zululand was quite unjustified. To the men on the spot, however, it was undertaken not to increase the bounds of the British Empire but as a protective measure for black and white alike against the greatest and most powerful warrior race Africa had ever known, who, it was believed, threatened the stability of an already highly volatile part of the world.

At first it was not such an uneven contest as might appear. On one side was the entire adult manhood of an African nation bred to conquest, disciplined, fearless, highly mobile and totally familiar with the terrain, yet armed largely with primitive weapons. On the other was a handful of regiments of British regular soldiers with some Colonial and African auxiliaries, armed with modern weapons, but gravely hampered by a lack of intelligence and problems of supply and transport. In matters of morale, steadfastness and endurance, there was little to choose between the two sides. Thus it came down to whether preponderance of numbers, speed of movement and warlike character could prevail against slow-moving firepower.

The high drama that resulted from the conflict between such diverse forces has been much written about, so it might well be asked if any further coverage is necessary. This book is offered in the hope that there may be many in whom an interest in the Zulu War has been whetted or renewed by its centenary, and others who would appreciate a picture of the campaign in more lasting and perhaps more truthful images than those possible in the more transient variety produced by film and television to mark the centenary.

By using old photographs of the scenes and protagonists, leavened by a few contemporary paintings, drawings and engravings of events and individuals, this book attempts to depict the war as it appeared to those who took part in it a hundred years ago. The accompanying text makes no claims to break new ground and serves merely to give a concise but complete account of the war, particularly of its less well-publicized events, so that the illustrations may be viewed in their proper context.

In finding the illustrations, as many collections as possible, both private and public, in South Africa as well as in the United Kingdom, have been consulted, with a particular view to originality. Owing to the limitations of photography at the time, not to mention the hazards of active service to the photographer, many of the photographs must of necessity be somewhat posed and wooden, hence the interspersion of a few paintings to add some movement to the over-all impression. Some of the pictures will inevitably be familiar to long-standing students of the Zulu War, but others will be less so and some have never been published before. For those who come fresh to the subject, the combination of words and pictures will, it is hoped, bring this now long-distant campaign to fresh life.

This number of illustrations could not have been assembled without the help of others. First I must mention Mr Ian Knight, who has made a considerable study of the campaign and the Zulus in particular; his friendly co-operation and advice have been consistently helpful and unfailingly unselfish. Mr R. J. Marrion most kindly searched his extensive collection of military photographs for suitable material. Some of the portraits of winners of the Victoria Cross have been made available by Mr Brian Best and Mr Keith Reeves from their collections. Among institutions in the United Kingdom I am indebted to the staff of the National Army Museum, London, who despite being impeded by building activities have met all requests with their usual courtesy; to Major G. T. Faulkner and the Buffs Museum Trustees and to Mr K. G. H. Reedie of the City of Canterbury Museum; to Lieutenant-Colonel A. C. M. Urwick of the Somerset Light Infantry section of the County Museum, Taunton; to Major G. E. Dodd of the Sherwood Foresters Museum; to Major G. J. B. Egerton of the South Wales Borderers Museum, especially for his assistance over the cover picture; and to the Curators of other museums of regiments involved in the war who obligingly replied to questions about their collections. Among South African institutions I am most grateful for their painstaking help to Mrs L. J. De Wet of the Africana Museum, Johannesburg, and to Mrs S. Bailey of the Local History Museum, Durban; to Commandant S. Bourquin for items from his collection; to the Killie Campbell Library, Durban; and to Miss I. M. Dugmore of the Fort Beaufort Historical Museum for suggestions and copies of the *South African Military History Journal*. To the publishers, Blandford Press, I must express my gratitude for bringing a long-conceived project to fruition, and in particular to Mr Barry Gregory for his friendly collaboration; also to my agent, Mrs Sheila Watson, for looking after my interests with her customary efficiency. Lastly I must record my appreciation of the forbearance of my wife and family, particularly of the former, who uncomplainingly spent many hours with me at a number of the places mentioned in these pages.

Jersey, C.I. (1979)   *M. J. B.*

Acknowledgements

The publishers gratefully acknowledge the following for permission to reproduce illustrations (figures refer to page numbers).

Africana Museum, Johannesburg: 7 (left), 9, 27 (top), 29 (top), 54, 55, 80, 81, 82, 83, 85 (bottom), 86, 89, 90 (bottom), 92 (bottom), 97, 103, 106, 107, 111, 114 (bottom), 117 (top), 122, 123 (top), 125 (bottom), 126 (top), 129, 131 (bottom), 132, 135, 141 (bottom), 150, 152, 155, 158 (bottom), 159, 162.

Killie Campbell Africana Library: 12, 16, 17, 20, 35, 127.

Local History Museum, Durban: 27 (bottom), 29 (bottom), 31, 33, 66 (top), 72, 78, 87, 90 (top), 94 (bottom), 100, 121 (left), 149, 166.

S. Bourquin Collection: 2, 57, 109 (top), 168.

National Army Museum, London: 4, 7 (top right), 19, 21, 22, 24, 25, 26, 28, 30, 34, 37 (bottom left), 41, 42, 46, 47, 52, 60, 64, 68, 69, 71, 73 (bottom), 85 (top), 88, 92 (top), 93, 95, 108, 109 (bottom), 110, 112, 113, 120 (top), 123 (bottom), 126 (bottom), 128, 130, 136, 137, 140, 141 (top right), 142, 143, 156, 157, 160, 167, 172–3.

The Buffs and Canterbury Royal Museums: 37 (top left), 90.

The Sherwood Foresters Museum: 37 (top right), 74, 101, 102, 121 (right).

The South Wales Borderers Museum: Cover, 63.

The Somerset Light Infantry and County Museum, Taunton: 104, 117 (bottom), 158 (top).

R. J. Marrion Collection: 49, 65, 120 (bottom), 125 (top), 131 (top), 133, 148.

Ian J. Knight Collection: 56, 58.

Brian Best Collection: 66 (bottom), 114 (top), 141 (top left).

Keith Reeves Collection: 70, 73 (top and centre).

Author's Collection: 59, 94 (top), 154.

PART I

THE COMING OF THE WAR

1

Britons, Boers and Bantus

A hundred years ago the biggest threat to the security of the British Empire was believed to be the expansion, outside Europe, of French and above all Russian influence. A particular concern of British ministers was the possible danger to the Crown's most treasured possession, India, caused by Russian advances in Central Asia, which in the late 1870s were growing ever closer to the kingdom of Afghanistan bordering on the North-West Frontier. To forestall the establishment of any Russian presence in that country, three columns of British and Indian troops crossed the Frontier, and by late January 1879 were firmly positioned in central Afghanistan. At the same time, over 5,000 miles away, three more British columns crossed another frontier, that of Cetshwayo, King of the Zulus, whose lands bordered on the British colony of Natal on the eastern seaboard of South Africa. In no way could this incursion be regarded as a counter-measure to French or Russian expansion, but its immediate causes had their distant origins in the same over-all Imperial policy as that which had initiated the invasion of Afghanistan, and which had preoccupied Britain throughout the nineteenth century – the security of India and Britain's communications with the sub-continent.

The seaward route to India round the Cape of Good Hope had been threatened during the French Revolutionary and Napoleonic Wars by France's defeat of the Dutch in 1794, whose harbours at the Cape were then opened to French men-of-war. To eliminate this threat Britain seized the Cape in 1795, but returned it to the Dutch after the Peace of Amiens in 1801. Five years later, with Napoleon swallowing up Europe, Britain again occupied the Cape and this time remained there to ensure that this vital link in the Imperial chain did not fall into unfriendly hands. At the time, the British Government had no wish to extend the limits of the colony which already, owing to the spread of Dutch settlers, extended 450 miles eastwards to the Great Fish River. The authorities at the Cape, however, found the peace of the territory threatened by Kaffir tribes raiding across the river, and two expeditions, in 1812 and 1819, had to be mounted to drive them out. Forts were built along the frontier, and immigrants from Britain were persuaded to settle in the eastern region of Cape Colony to swell the European population.

The tribes the British encountered on the Fish River were the vanguard of a great black wave of Bantu peoples which had been pressing down eastern Africa for over two centuries. This movement found itself halted on the frontier of Cape Colony, but at the same time the tribes in the lead were coming under increasing pressure from their rear. In 1816 Shaka, the king of a once-small Bantu clan, the Zulus, began a career of conquest against all the neighbouring

1

tribes. By turning his tribe into a military machine and pursuing his aims with a ruthless savagery, he made the Zulus into the most powerful and feared race in South Africa, a quarter of a million strong, whose conquered territories, by 1824, stretched from the Pongola River into central Natal and from the coast to the Drakensberg mountains. Shaka's first contact with the British came the same year, when Francis Farewell and Henry Fynn landed in Natal with the view to establishing a trading settlement at Port Natal, later Durban. Shaka developed a liking for them and agreed to their project. The two Englishmen hoodwinked him into signing a document, which he could not read, and which ceded to them the outright title to Durban and 3,500 square miles of the surrounding countryside. Farewell proclaimed the area as British territory, but the Governor of Cape Colony had more than enough to contend with on his eastern frontier without extending his responsibilities into Natal. Indeed in 1834 he was confronted with a further uprising in Kaffraria, after which the frontier was pushed up to the Kei River.

Meanwhile Shaka had been murdered in 1828 by his half-brother Dingane, who, once he had seized the throne, displayed none of Shaka's lust for conquest but gave himself over to self-indulgence. He continued Shaka's policy of friendliness towards the British settlement at Durban which, despite mixed fortunes, continued to attract more settlers and some missionaries, until by 1834 it contained some fifty Europeans. Then a new factor entered the scene. In 1835 the Boers in Cape Colony, finding their traditional way of life frustrated by the British administration, began their Great Trek northwards in search of new lands. After defeating the Basuto and Matabele tribes who opposed their advance, some of the Boers established themselves in what later became the Orange Free State and the Transvaal. Others, attracted by the far more fertile land to the east, made their way in 1837 over the Drakensberg mountains into Natal where their leader, Piet

Zulu warriors of two of Mpande's favourite regiments in 1846: Isanqu, or AmaShishi, on left; inDabakawombe on right. Painting by Angas.

Retief, sought Dingane's permission to settle. Dingane agreed, subject to Retief's recapturing some Zulu cattle stolen by a Basuto chief. When Retief and sixty Boers returned to Dingane's kraal in February 1838 with the cattle, the Zulu king massacred them all and sent his warriors out to destroy the remaining Boers, their wives and their children, of whom only a few escaped back over the Drakensberg. Prior to the massacre some of the British settlers at Durban had made common cause with the Boers and now, alarmed at this outburst of savagery, marched with some Bantu levies to their aid, but were annihilated in their turn. Dingane's warriors then launched themselves against Durban, where the remaining settlers just managed to escape by ship. The settlement was sacked and the Zulus retired back over the River Tugela.

The British authorities both at the Cape and at home had viewed the trekking of the Boers with disfavour, not simply because they were British subjects but for fear of the native unrest such a movement was likely to stir up. The events in Natal in 1838 had proved such fears to be well founded. Although unwilling to annex Natal, they realized that the massacre of Piet Retief's men would inevitably drive the Boers to avenge the murders, and indeed they were already moving back into Natal. Action to prevent any further outbreak of trouble was at first restricted to an embargo on the traffic of arms to Natal but, pressed by the Governor of Cape Colony, the Colonial Office in London agreed to the despatch of a small force of troops to Durban. When these arrived in early December 1838, their commander, Major Charters of the Royal Artillery, found that the Boers had already annexed the settlement in May and set up their own republic. He also learned that they had been preparing a punitive expedition under Andreas Pretorius against the Zulus. He immediately sent orders to Pretorius not to move, but he was too late. On 16 December, 12,000 Zulus threw themselves against Pretorius' wagon laager on the Blood River, only to be mown down by the Boers' muskets and cannon. After two hours' ceaseless charges, 3,000 Zulus had been killed and the rest fled, mercilessly pursued by the Boers. The victorious commando returned to Natal into which the trekkers now poured, setting up the capital of their republic at Pietermaritzburg, some 50 miles inland and north-west of Durban.

At the latter place the British garrison still remained but, faced with a fresh influx of Boers into Natal, there was little Charters could do to assert his authority. His successor, Captain Jarvis, patched up a treaty with Dingane and in December 1839, with the new Boer republic seemingly peacefully established,

the British garrison withdrew from Durban, which the Boers occupied.

The latter, however, would never feel secure while Dingane still ruled to their north. Their opportunity to dispose of him once and for all arose when his half-brother, Mpande, fearful for his life, fled from Zululand with 17,000 followers into Natal. The Boers and Mpande struck a bargain: he would return to Zululand if the Boers assisted him to overthrow Dingane. In January 1840 Dingane was defeated and fled to Swaziland where, deserted by his followers, he was killed. The Boers installed the amiable and pacific Mpande as King of the Zulus, settling as their border with Zululand the Tugela, exacting a levy of several thousand head of cattle, and seizing a thousand Zulu youths, who were put into domestic service.

Zululand under Mpande was now quiet, but at Cape Town and in London there was concern about Natal. The Boers' attack on Dingane was seen as aggression by people still considered as British subjects against a chief with whom the British had signed a treaty. The Boer treatment of the tribes in Kaffraria was not conducive to peace on the eastern frontier of the Cape, and indeed their whole attitude to the native races as a source of cheap labour, if not as slaves, contravened laws passed in Cape Colony in 1807 by the British, which gave all races equality before the law — one of the prime factors that had sparked off the Great Trek. The Boer administration in Natal was proving increasingly inept and, altogether, the chances of stability in the area seemed slight. In August 1841 further high-handed action against the natives in southern Natal finally convinced the British that action could no longer be deferred. A small force of British troops, chiefly of the 27th Regiment under Captain Smith, marched north, and in May 1842 reoccupied Durban. Within three weeks he was besieged by the Boers, who by their action were now in open rebellion against the Crown. Smith held out for 34 days until reinforcements arrived from the Cape to raise the siege, and the Boers withdrew.

Cetshwayo, King of the Zulus, 1873–79.

The British Government now decided to annex Natal as a colony, and a High Commissioner was appointed to negotiate with the Boers. Hoping for a considerable degree of autonomy, which the Commissioner in fact later recommended to London, the Boers yielded. They were to be disappointed, however, for in 1845 Natal was formally annexed, not as a separate colony, but as a district of Cape Colony under a lieutenant-governor, with legislative power in the hands of the Governor at the Cape. As the territory settled down to a period of peace at last, more British settlers moved in and most of the Boers moved out. To the north, Mpande was eager to come to terms with the British. Having promised that the Zulus would remain north of the Tugela and east of the Buffalo, and also ceding the use of St Lucia Bay, over 100 miles up the coast of Zululand, he obtained a treaty from them. With every harbour around the south-east coast of Africa between Cape Town and Delagoa Bay now in British hands, their use would be denied to any unfriendly power. Nevertheless, naval supremacy in the Indian Ocean off southern Africa could only be maintained if the hinterland of the coastal strip on which it depended was kept tranquil and orderly.

This tranquillity was threatened on the eastern Cape frontier in 1847 and again in 1850 by the native uprisings known as the Seventh and Eighth Kaffir Wars. From Natal most of the Boers moved into the area between the Orange and Vaal Rivers, but in 1847 they decided to move north again over the Vaal when Sir Harry Smith, Governor at the Cape, annexed the former territory as the Orange River Sovereignty. Five years later, however, the Boers north of the Vaal were granted their freedom from British jurisdiction, setting up their own republic of the Transvaal; and in 1854 the British relinquished the Orange River Sovereignty which became a second Boer republic as the Orange Free State. Between 1848 and 1851, over 3,000 British immigrants arrived to settle in Natal, but, against this, many of the natives driven out by the Zulus began to return, and by the mid-1850s there were over 150,000 Natal Kaffirs in the colony.

Zululand under Mpande remained quiet and undisturbed by either Boer or Briton. Mpande had two sons born of different mothers: the eldest, but, under Zulu custom, not necessarily the heir, was Cetshwayo, and the other was Mbulazi. Mpande exercised a much looser control than Shaka over his nation. As the boys grew up, various elements began to attach themselves to each son with an eye to the future after Mpande's death. Cetshwayo's followers, the uSuthu, outnumbered Mbulazi's by three to one. In 1856, when Cetshwayo was about thirty and the succession was still undecided, matters came to a head when the uSuthu attacked and overwhelmed Mbulazi with great slaughter on the Tugela. With Mbulazi out of the way, Cetshwayo began to consolidate his position as the most obvious heir, eliminating any other possible rivals and assuming more and more control over the whole kingdom. To ensure further his succession, he realized that he would have to cultivate friendly relations with both the Boers in the Transvaal and the British in Natal, but, appreciating the hostility between the two, he decided to play one off against the other.

For their part, the British in Natal and in particular the Secretary for Native Affairs, Theophilus Shepstone, viewed the rise of the new star in Zululand with some alarm. A strong and powerful king in Zululand, if hostile, would pose a most dangerous threat to the colony, whereas an alliance between the Zulus and Boers might give the latter access to the coast, from which it was policy to exclude them. Shepstone therefore set out to win Cetshwayo's friendship, which he did by recognizing him as the heir-apparent in the name of the Queen. Cetshwayo was delighted with this support, but the goodwill thus generated was then marred by Shepstone's announcement that such recognition was only granted conditionally on Cetshwayo's proper conduct in the future.

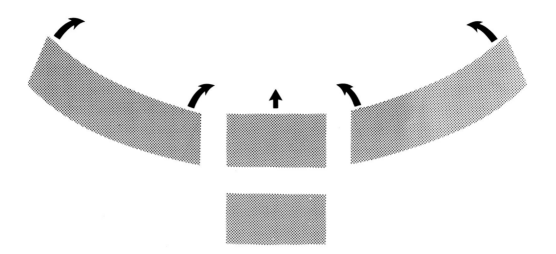

Cetshwayo enforced strict discipline in the field of battle as well as the military kraal. The Zulu impi comprised a horde of warriors deploying in two huge enveloping horns from the chest or headquarter body in the centre and supported by the loins or reserve in the rear of the chest.

In 1872 Mpande died. Cetshwayo knew that there were still relatives who could threaten his succession and he was distrustful of both British and Boer intentions towards Zululand, but without a powerful sponsor he could not be sure of the throne. In turning to the British, with an invitation to Shepstone to crown him as King of the Zulus in the Queen's name, he hoped for support and protection without domination. Shepstone was ready to comply, not only to ensure a friendly Zululand on Natal's northern border, but also as the first stage towards obtaining eventual control over the country. During the coronation at the royal kraal at Ulundi he again emphasized the principles he expected Cetshwayo to abide by in his reign.

Cetshwayo listened, but with the throne now secure and the Zulus acknowledging his kingship, he had no intention of ruling to the dictates of an outsider. Nevertheless, Shepstone returned to Natal, confident that Zululand was in good hands. Cetshwayo was about forty-five,

a fine and commanding figure, tall and well-built, though with a tendency to the corpulence of his forebears. Unlike his easy-going father, he was energetic, ambitious to become a worthy successor to the great Shaka and, though completely illiterate, possessed of an intelligence and grasp of affairs uncommon in a savage of his background and time. He was suspicious of Europeans, particularly the Boers, but not unnaturally lacked the sophistication to understand their political manoeuvres. He was determined, now he had the throne, to assert his authority over his people, retain his independence, and restore the prestige of the Zulus to that of former times, but not at the expense of his European neighbours with whom he was willing to live in peace. He maintained a force of 50,000 men under arms, organized in the strictly disciplined military system he had inherited from his forebears. Though he may have had no aggressive intentions outside his borders, he fully realized that such a formidable

Top Left: Sir Theophilus Shepstone, Secretary for Native Affairs in Natal and Administrator of the Transvaal from 1877.

Bottom Left: Sir Bartle Frere, Governor of Cape Colony and High Commissioner for Native Affairs in South Africa.

Top Right: Frederick Augustus Thesiger, 2nd Baron Chelmsford. Lieutenant-General commanding British forces in South Africa, 1878–79.

array made him a power to be reckoned with in dealings with his neighbours. On the other hand, this army contained within its system the seeds of trouble which could bend its ruler and commander to its will. Shaka had laid down: 'Marriage for young warriors is folly. Their first and last duty is to protect the interests of the nation. This they cannot do efficiently if they have family ties.' All the young warriors were therefore kept in enforced celibacy until they reached the age of forty or until their prowess in battle, either individually or collectively as a regiment, earned them their king's permission to marry. Only by war, therefore, and the chance to wash their spears in blood, could the warriors escape the imprisonment of their celibacy. The urge to fight was thus strongly heightened in a people already warlike by nature; but, although it gave the king a military arm of immense bravery and ferocity, it was not conducive to the policy of peaceful co-existence Cetshwayo intended to pursue on assuming the throne.

The chief external problem facing Cetshwayo was a dispute over an area east of the Blood River, which the Transvaal Boers claimed had been ceded to them by Mpande; Cetshwayo denied this, seeking the support of the British in his cause. The policy of the British Government at this time towards South Africa was that, for economic reasons and in order to solve the besetting problems of drought, cattle disease and land hunger, the different territories should be linked in a confederation. This would include the Boer republics which now, following the discovery therein of gold and diamonds, included numbers of British subjects. A conference held in London in 1876 foundered owing to the differences and antagonisms of the various territories. The following year the Transvaal failed to subdue an uprising by a rebellious chief, Sekukuni. Alarmed at the possible effect of Sekukuni's success upon the rest of black Africa, and particularly the Zulus, Lord Carnarvon, the Colonial Secretary, empowered Shepstone to annex the Transvaal. This he achieved, though by rather dubious

means, but in so doing put paid to any hope of confederation, since the Orange Free State now feared for its own independence. Furthermore, by assuming the administration of the Transvaal, Shepstone had become responsible for the problem of the territory on the Blood River disputed between the Boers and Cetshwayo.

Meanwhile Carnarvon, in an effort to push through confederation, had appointed Sir Bartle Frere as Governor of Cape Colony and High Commissioner for Native Affairs in South Africa. Frere was now sixty-two and had had a distinguished career as a civil servant in India. As Governor of Scinde he had kept that province quiet during the Sepoy Mutiny, and was later Governor of Bombay. He was extremely able and hard-working; but his experience in India, where a highly-trained, largely European civil service presided autocratically, if benevolently, over mainly biddable and quiescent native masses, had bred in him a way of thought and action which would not be appropriate in southern Africa, with its various territories, and its sizeable, individualistic and frequently mutually antagonistic European races, living uneasily amid a sea of volatile Africans.

Frere had not long arrived in South Africa before he had a full-scale native uprising on his hands – the Ninth Kaffir War, which broke out in 1878. Although this was indicative of the general restlessness of the native races, it had no bearing or effect on the problems of Natal, the Transvaal and Zululand, other than the emergence on the scene of a figure who was later to play a major part in events in those areas. In March 1878 there arrived at Cape Town to assume command of all forces in South Africa, Lieutenant-General the Honourable Sir Frederick Augustus Thesiger. The son of Lord Chelmsford, Thesiger was then aged fifty, having begun his military career in 1844 in the Rifle Brigade, transferring a year later to the Grenadier Guards. In 1858 he had exchanged into the 95th Regiment, commanding it in the

Sir Bartle Frere's ultimatum being read to Cetshwayo's emissaries at the Lower Tugela Drift, 11 December 1878.

later stages of the Sepoy Mutiny, and thereafter had served on the staff in India and during the Abyssinian campaign of 1868. He was a tall, distinguished figure with all the attributes of the Victorian officer and gentleman, and was regarded by his contemporaries as a somewhat colourless and highly reserved character, but nevertheless perfectly competent and reliable. In the Ninth Kaffir War he found himself commanding not only British regular troops but also colonial and native levies of a type and discipline of which he had no experience; he managed to earn their respect and confidence, and generally was considered to have conducted a successful campaign. Frere found him entirely satisfactory, quite content to confine himself to military matters and to leave political affairs in the Governor's hands.

Frere quickly appreciated that the underlying cause of all unrest in South Africa was land ownership. The minority Europeans, whether Boer or British, occupied the best and most fertile lands, while the native tribes were being crammed into less favourable areas, where the ever-present threat of drought, primitive agricultural methods and cattle disease made their living precarious. Only by confederation of all the territories, with a unified land and native policy, could stability be achieved. Frere realized that the Boers were likely to prove intransigent, but with the Transvaal now annexed he hoped that any difficulties with them could be overcome. His eye, however, was increasingly drawn towards Zululand. Despite Sekukuni's revolt, now being put down by British troops, and the Ninth Kaffir War, Cetshwayo had kept the Zulus quiet, but clearly confederation could not succeed while an independent, savage nation with a large and powerful army existed in its midst, giving inspiration to the subject native races. Sooner or later Zululand would have to be annexed or at least made to accept British supervision of its affairs. Sir Henry Bulwer, the Lieutenant-

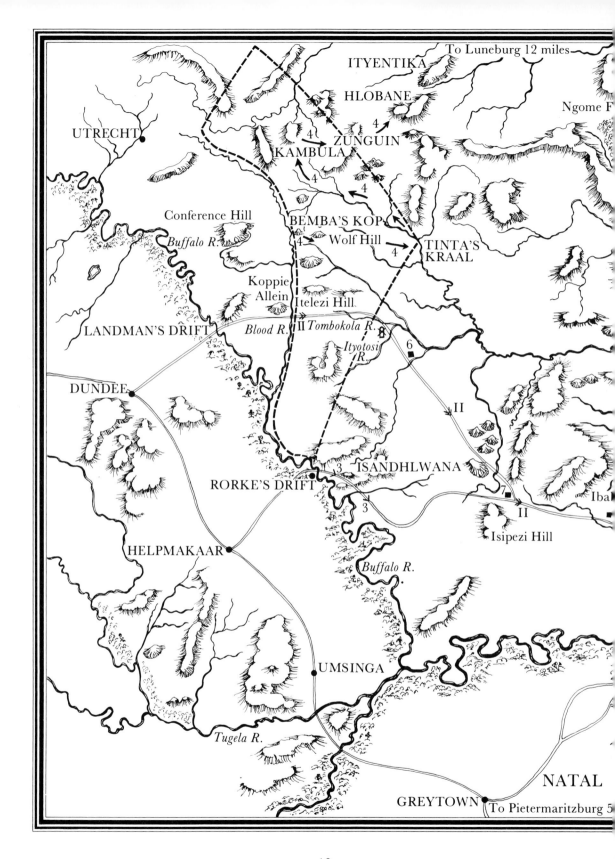

ITYENTIKA

HLOBANE

To Luneburg 12 miles

Ngome F

UTRECHT

4 ZUNGUIN 4

KAMBULA

4

4

Conference Hill

BEMBA'S KOP

Buffalo R.

4 Wolf Hill

4

TINTA'S KRAAL

Koppie Allein

Itelezi Hill

LANDMAN'S DRIFT

Blood R. II Tombokola R. 8

Ityotosi R.

6

DUNDEE

II

3 ISANDHLWANA

RORKE'S DRIFT

7

3

II

Iba

Isipezi Hill

HELPMAKAAR

Buffalo R.

UMSINGA

Tugela R.

NATAL

GREYTOWN

To Pietermaritzburg 5

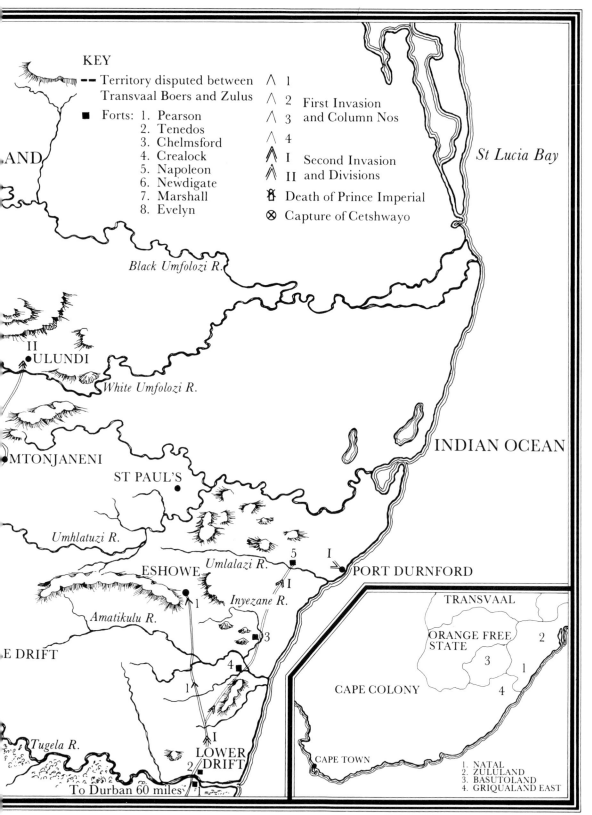

AND

Black Umfolozi R.

II
●ULUNDI

White Umfolozi R.

●MTONJANENI

ST PAUL'S ●

Umhlatuzi R.

ESHOWE

Umlalazi R.

Inyezane R.

Amatikulu R.

E DRIFT

5 ■
I →
I

1

3 ■

4 ■

1

I
LOWER
DRIFT

Tugela R.

2 ■

To Durban 60 miles

St Lucia Bay

INDIAN OCEAN

I →
PORT DURNFORD

TRANSVAAL

ORANGE FREE
STATE   2

3   1

CAPE COLONY   4

CAPE TOWN

1. NATAL
2. ZULULAND
3. BASUTOLAND
4. GRIQUALAND EAST

Northern Natal and Zululand, showing outline of operations.

Front and back views of a Zulu warrior in full ceremonial regalia. Note the headdress of brown fur skull cap, leopard-skin headband and feathers, plus the cowtails spread over chest and back. The lack of a headring and the black shield with one white spot indicate an unmarried regiment.

Governor of Natal, counselled restraint and caution towards Cetshwayo, but Frere became increasingly obsessed by this potential powder keg.

Events were now accelerated by the situation in the Transvaal. Shepstone's administration was foundering and the Boers were becoming restless, as much affected by land hunger as were the Bantu races. In an attempt to placate the Boers, Shepstone relinquished his earlier support for Cetshwayo's claim to the disputed territory on the Blood River and espoused the Boer cause. This change of heart by one he had always regarded as his friend alarmed Cetshwayo, who appealed to Bulwer to arbitrate in the matter. Bulwer agreed, and with the support of Frere, who had been convinced by Shepstone of the justice of the Boer claims, set up a Boundary Commission. In June 1878 the Commission reported, but its findings were a bombshell to Frere. Contrary to his expectations it found no justification whatsoever in the Boer claim and unreservedly reccmmended that the whole Blood River area as far north as the Boer settlement at Utrecht inclusive be returned to the Zulus. Frere was appalled, for he believed that such findings, once made public, could not only provoke a revolt in the Transvaal, but might also spark off a Zulu attack on the Boers which in turn could incite a general native uprising. To gain time he sent off the Commission's report to the Colonial Office in London, and in the meantime instructed Thesiger to prepare a military appreciation of how best to deal with Zululand, should this become necessary. He then went north to confer with Bulwer in Natal.

By now Frere had more or less convinced himself that the only hope for stability was to strike at the Zulus before they rose in arms, but his hands were tied for the time being by Thesiger's disclosure that the forces in South Africa were insufficient for such an enterprise. Furthermore he found in Bulwer, from whose province such a military operation would have to be mounted, a man who took a very different view of events. Bulwer was unable to countenance any action against Cetshwayo who, he maintained, had done nothing to disturb the peace or threaten British interests. He agreed that, once the Commission's findings were published, the Boers in the disputed territories, who since Shepstone's annexation were British subjects, might be in danger. If they chose not to remain under Zulu rule, as clearly it would be unwise for them to do, they should be compensated for the loss of their land, but he thought that such compensation should come from the Transvaal. Frere, on the other hand, was adamant that any compensation should come from the Zulus.

He next took issue with Bulwer over a number of incidents that had occurred in Zululand, or on its border with Natal. At least two of these stemmed from the head of steam building up within the unmarried and celibate Zulu regiments who had been denied the chance to wash their spears by Cetshwayo's peaceful policies. Disputes over women had led to bloodshed which Cetshwayo had punished by summary execution of the perpetrators. When Bulwer learned of one of these incidents, he chided Cetshwayo, reminding him of Shepstone's warning at his coronation, particularly those against indiscriminate killing. Cetshwayo replied hotly that Shepstone may have instructed but he had given no undertaking to abide by those instructions. He emphasized his independence, saying he would rule according to his laws. He said, not without

justification: 'Why does the Governor of Natal speak to me about my laws? Do I go to Natal and dictate to him about his laws? While wishing to be friends with the English I do not agree to give my people over to be governed by laws sent to me by them.' Bulwer accepted this reply without demur, recognizing it as a natural reaction. Many of the alarmist rumours reaching him from Zululand came from missionaries. Cetshwayo did not welcome their attempts to convert his people, which were largely unsuccessful, but at the same time no missionary had come to any harm at Zulu hands. Some of their converts, however, were killed. Again Bulwer was not disposed to interfere, since the missionaries' activities had always been outside his jurisdiction. In July 1878 two wives of a Zulu chief, Sihayo, absconded with their lovers into Natal. A party of Zulus crossed the border, recaptured the women and once back in Zululand executed them. Bulwer was not prepared to let this incursion go unpunished and requested extradition of the raiders for trial in Natal. Cetshwayo agreed that the raiders should be punished, but since they had not killed on Natal soil and the women had broken Zulu law he was reluctant to order their extradition. When Frere heard of this he was furious, vehemently disagreeing with Bulwer, who regarded these incidents as the normal consequences of living cheek-by-jowl with an unsophisticated people. Frere maintained that they were indicative of the savagery of the Zulus and therefore of the imminent danger in which Natal stood.

Frere had long since reported to London Thesiger's conclusions about the shortages of troops and his request for at least two more battalions and some cavalry to be sent out from England. By November he had received not only the Colonial Secretary's endorsement of the Boundary Commission's report but also the unwelcome news that no reinforcements would be forthcoming and that Natal must be responsible for its own defence with its own resources. Frere therefore insisted to Bulwer

13

that Thesiger, now Lord Chelmsford since the death of his father the previous month, must raise and train 7,000 native levies from the Natal Kaffirs to reinforce the British regular troops and colonial volunteer units in the colony. Bulwer reluctantly had to agree. This done, Frere felt ready to deal with Cetshwayo. The Zulu king was informed that the findings of the Boundary Commission would be announced at the Lower Drift of the Tugela River on 11 December 1878.

On that day Cetshwayo's emissaries were told that Zulu sovereignty over the Blood River territory was fully recognized but that – and here Frere's own hand was at work – the Boers who chose to leave were to be compensated by the Zulus, and those who stayed would be protected by the Crown with a British Resident at Utrecht. The emissaries accepted this with mixed feelings, but there was more to come. First, the perpetrators of the border incidents were to be surrendered within twenty days and two fines totalling 600 head of cattle for such incidents were to be paid within the same period. Within thirty days, summary executions without trial were to cease; the Zulu Army was to be disbanded and their military system broken up; all Zulus were to be free to marry on reaching maturity; missionaries and converts were not to be interfered with; a British Resident would be located in Zululand to enforce these requirements; no one was to be expelled from Zululand without the Resident's permission; and any dispute involving a European was to be heard in the presence of the King and the Resident.

It is difficult to guess who was the more flabbergasted at this ultimatum – Sir Michael Hicks Beach, now the Colonial Secretary in London, or Cetshwayo. The former, already alarmed at the line Frere had been taking at a time when war with Russia over Afghanistan was threatening, had earlier despatched a positive order against any invasion of Zululand, which did not reach Frere until two days after the ultimatum to the Zulus had been announced. He did, however, relent on the question of the reinforcements, and two battalions were ordered out. The terms of the ultimatum were not in Hicks Beach's hand until 2 January 1879, by which time he knew it was too late to prevent Frere taking action. As for the wretched Cetshwayo, he was bewildered at this sudden turn of events. Apprehensive of confronting the King and delayed by flooded rivers, the emissaries made slow progress to Ulundi, but news of the ultimatum reached Cetshwayo through John Dunn, a white settler who had lived in Zululand for years and enjoyed his confidence. To Cetshwayo and his chiefs the demands for the surrender of the malefactors, even the cattle fines, were understandable if unpalatable and unreasonable, but the other clauses which threatened Zululand's independence and way of life seemed so outrageous that they were barely considered.

On 18 December, Cetshwayo sent word that he would hand over the men and cattle but that it would take time to round them up and get them to the border across the flooded rivers; he appealed for no action to be taken should they not arrive before the twenty days were up. Frere dismissed this plea as evasive tactics on Cetshwayo's part, and replied that, if his terms were not complied with by the time stipulated, his troops would enter Zululand at the end of the twenty days, but that they would not advance until the full thirty days had passed. On 4 January, no further communication from Cetshwayo having been received, Frere informed Chelmsford that the enforcement of the demands was now in his hands, and on the 11th Chelmsford's forces crossed the border into Zululand. Frere got the action he desired and for which Chelmsford had been preparing since arriving in Natal the previous August.

2

The Opposing Forces

High among Chelmsford's concerns when he had arrived in Natal to consider the military problems of dealing with Zululand had been the strength and capabilities of the Zulu Army. Fortunately a border agent, H. B. Fynney, had long been making a study of the Zulu military system, and the information he had accumulated provided Chelmsford with a comprehensive and detailed survey of what he would be up against if military action became necessary.

The Zulu nation in the late 1870s maintained nearly 50,000 men under arms. Military service was required of Zulu males from late adolescence until they were no longer physically capable of bearing arms; thus there were men in their sixties and even seventies in their ranks. Each warrior was possessed of a naturally warlike spirit, a ready obedience and submission to his elders under the pain of dire punishment, and a conviction of his own invincibility, stemming from mental and physical preparation for war by the witch doctors. They were tall, strong and, because of their early upbringing in which they were always out of doors tending cattle and hunting, of great hardiness and endurance. To these attributes was added a high skill with their weapons, to which they had been accustomed since an early age.

These consisted primarily of the assegai and shield. Before Shaka's time the Bantu had used a throwing spear, but Shaka had forbidden it in favour of a short, stabbing weapon, the 'iXwa', which had a blade 18 inches long and about $1\frac{1}{2}$ inches wide, fastened to a 30-inch shaft. This spear had remained the chief Zulu weapon ever since, although a lighter type had come into use, and the throwing spear had made a reappearance as an additional weapon. Shields were made of stiffened cowhide in an oval shape and were attached to a pole by a strip of hide laced through a series of slots, with a fur crest on top of the pole and a leather thong on the inner side. They came in two sizes: the war shield, or 'isiHlangu', of Shaka's day was 2 ft 6 in wide and between 4 ft 6 in and 6 ft high, depending on the warrior's height; and a smaller, handier version, introduced by Cetshwayo in the 1850s, was about 3 ft 6 in high and 2 ft wide. Warriors were trained to wield shield and assegai in conjunction, using the former first to deflect an opponent's thrust and then to hook it under his shield, pulling him off balance and leaving him defenceless against the upward thrust of the 'iXwa'. Some Zulus favoured the club-like knobkerrie. Firearms had been reaching Zululand during the two decades prior to the war, either smuggled in from Natal, bought from the Portuguese colonies, or looted from the Boers; many more were taken from British casualties after the war began. With the exception of a few marksmen, however, the Zulus never became adept at musketry, their firepower being usually more noticeable for its

Zulu chief of a black shield regiment.

6,000, but the average strength of each in 1879 was around 1,500. The regiments lived in special military kraals where new regiments would be linked with older formations to form a larger organization roughly approximating to a brigade or even a corps, so that young warriors could gain experience from their elders. The Undi Corps, for example, consisted of five regiments, three of which (uThulwane, Nkonkone and Ndhlondhlo) ranged in age from forty-three to forty-five, one, inDluyengwe, of men of twenty-eight, and the other, inGobamakhosi, of younger men aged twenty-four, totalling 9,900 men in all. As mentioned in the previous chapter, the warriors of young regiments were kept in enforced celibacy, usually until they were aged about forty, when whole regiments were given permission to marry at the same time. Married men became known as 'iKhehla' and wore the 'isiCoco', a fibre circlet woven into the hair.

The age and experience of different regiments were also marked by the shield colour: young regiments had black shields which were allowed to acquire white markings as their experience increased; red shields denoted married or mixed regiments; seniority and battle experience were signified by shields of increasing whiteness until the final dignity of an all-white shield was achieved. The basic dress of the warrior was the 'umuTsha', a string worn round the waist from which strips of fur hung down in front and a strip of cowhide at the back. Senior regiments wore a kilt of fur and hide tails over the umuTsha. The warrior was further adorned by elaborate arrangements of fur, hide and feathers worn round the head, neck, arms and below the knees, all of which served not only to enhance his ferocious aspect but also to distinguish one regiment from another. The umHlanga regiment, for example, wore a leopard-skin headband, black ostrich feathers in front surmounted by longer white feathers, green monkey-skin earflaps, white cowtail necklace over chest and back, and carried a black shield with one white spot on the lower half. Much of

volume than its accuracy, and their possession of firearms seldom influenced their traditional battle tactics and preference for close-quarter combat. They never had any artillery, nor was any part of their army mounted.

Before being assimilated into the army proper, young Zulu boys were formed by age and district into groups about a hundred strong called 'iNtanga' under a leader, or 'inDuna', of a slightly older age-group. When the boys of various iNtangas reached military age, their units were formed into a regiment, all of the same age-group and district, under the inDuna of the senior iNtanga. The strength of a regiment might vary from 500 to as many as

Warriors of various Zulu regiments in war regalia.

the adornment was reserved for ceremonial occasions and not worn on active service, but enough fur and feather remained so that, in conjunction with a man's shield colour, age and whether he wore the isiCoco, his regiment could always be determined.

In 1879 the Zulu Army consisted of thirty-three regiments, but since seven of these dated from the days of Shaka and Dingane and their age-group ranged from sixty-four to eighty their numbers and their effectiveness were slight. Eighteen of the regiments consisted of married men. All were grouped into thirteen 'corps', varying in strength from the five-regiment Undi already mentioned to the uDukuza of one 75-year-old regiment and the 500-strong Iqwa. The corps organization was, however, more administrative than operational and in battle a regiment might fight with another corps not from its own kraal.

A Zulu army, or 'impi', was rapidly mobilized for war when the king despatched runners to order the assembly of the regiments at their respective kraals and their subsequent concentration at the royal kraal. Unencumbered by anything but their shields and assegais, an impi could cover 40–50 miles a day, unimpeded by the difficulties of terrain that so hindered the movement of more sophisticated armies. Only a flooded river might delay their advance and then the impi would, as it were, charge the obstacle in a dense column with arms linked, relying on the momentum of the rush to carry all across when the leaders got out of their depth. Inevitably some were drowned but the majority surged through it. A few supplies for immediate use, together with cooking utensils and spare weapons, would be carried by parties of boys following the impi; further food and necessities would be gathered from kraals through which the impi passed. On arrival at the king's kraal the regiments underwent various rituals performed by the witch doctors to protect each individual warrior and to strengthen the impi as a whole, after which they were ready for action. After a battle

17

the men of an impi were subjected to various purification ceremonies.

Zulu tactics had remained unchanged since Shaka's day. When near to the enemy, the inDuna in chief command of the impi would give out his orders to the whole impi assembled around him in a circle, and then take up his position on a prominent feature as the army formed for battle. This it did by splitting into four divisions, prior to deploying into the attack formation based on the head of a charging buffalo: two divisions formed the wings or horns, one the centre or chest, while the fourth formed a reserve known as the loins; the latter was located behind the chest and was faced away from the action to prevent its warriors getting over-excited at the sight of their comrades fighting and charging prematurely. On a given signal the chest would advance and engage the enemy closely to fix him in position, while the horns would circle round to attack from flanks and rear. The reserve would be committed as and when the chief inDuna thought fit. Such tactics against native foes had usually proved overwhelming, but the Boers had shown at Blood River in 1838 that relatively small numbers of determined men armed with muskets and cannon, and entrenched behind a wagon laager, could put an impi to flight. The Zulus, however, had learned no lesson from that defeat and continued to put all their faith in the speed and savage courage of massed warriors, hacking and stabbing at close quarters in the charging buffalo formation.

If the effectiveness of the Zulu military machine was limited by their adherence to this one battlefield manoeuvre, even more so were their efforts affected by a lack of any over-all strategic plan. There was no deception, no attempt to lure an enemy into a trap, strike at his weak points and communications, or outflank him so as to thrust past him into his undefended rear areas, or even harass and wear him down by guerrilla tactics. The army was merely assembled into one great striking force and then hurled at the nearest suitable target. Furthermore, when a victory was won, there was no attempt to exploit it, nor was exploitation even possible, for the first priority after battle was the purification ceremonies to be carried out in their home kraals. There the regiments would remain until messengers summoned them again to the king's kraal. Thus to the Zulu mind the concept of a planned campaign was unknown, and warfare, whether offensive or defensive, was simply a series of bloody encounters. Nevertheless, for all its limitations, the Zulu Army contained magnificent material, its regiments were drilled and disciplined in their fighting methods, and it would be a foolish commander, however superior and sophisticated his own forces, who underestimated its prowess.

Against the Zulu array, Chelmsford could muster a mixed bag of troops. First, there were the regulars of the British Army garrisons in South Africa, infantry, artillery and supporting services but no cavalry; these could be supplemented by landing parties of sailors and marines from H.M. Ships in South African waters. For mounted troops he would have to rely on the European irregulars of the volunteer units from Natal and Cape Colony, plus the para-military Mounted Police. These two sources seemed inadequate for the task of both defending Natal and defeating the Zulus, so that when the request for reinforcements was turned down by the Colonial Office, the decision to raise native levies from the Natal Kaffirs was taken, thus forming the third element of Chelmsford's force.

When Chelmsford first began his military appreciation of the situation in August 1878, he found that, of British regulars, he only had immediately available in Natal and the Transvaal five battalions: the 2nd Battalion of the 3rd Regiment, the Buffs, the 1st Battalion 13th Light Infantry, the 1st and 2nd Battalions of the 24th Regiment, and the single battalion 90th Light Infantry. Part of the 1/24th was still in Cape Colony, mopping up after the Ninth

Kaffir War. The 80th Regiment was also in the Transvaal on the northern Zululand border at Luneburg but would have to remain there to protect that area and to keep an eye on the Boers. The 88th Regiment was in Cape Colony with companies detached as far afield as Mauritius and St Helena. When Frere's ultimatum to Cetshwayo forced the Colonial Secretary's hand over the matter of reinforcements, Chelmsford received from England the 2nd Battalion of the 4th King's Own and the 99th Regiment, giving him a total of seven battalions for action against the Zulus. In addition he had two batteries of Royal Artillery, and two companies of Royal Engineers were on the way, although one would arrive too late for the initial operations.

In 1879 the 109 regiments of Infantry of the Line were still known by their numbers, although most had a subsidiary title – the 13th, for example, being 1st Somersetshire Prince Albert's, and the 24th being 2nd Warwickshires. All regiments had only one battalion, except the first twenty-five which each had two. The designation of Light Infantry borne by the 13th and 90th was an honorary distinction and had no tactical or organizational significance. An infantry battalion at its war establishment was supposed to have a total of 31 officers, 50 staff sergeants and sergeants, 41 corporals, 16 drummers (or buglers for Light Infantry) and 959 privates (including bandsmen, pioneers and drivers), a total of 1,097 all ranks. At the beginning of the Zulu War, however, the battalions were on the Field Force, South Africa establishment, which by a reduction in the number of privates gave a strength of 896 all told, the higher ranks remaining more or less unchanged from the war establishment. The battalion was organized into a headquarters and eight lettered companies. The headquarters included, in officers, the lieutenant-colonel commanding, two majors, the adjutant, quartermaster, medical officer and paymaster, the latter usually remaining at the base of operations; its N.C.O.s consisted of the sergeant-major, the quartermaster-sergeant, bandmaster, and seven sergeants or staff sergeants with specialist duties – orderly-room clerk, drum-major, armourer, pay clerk, cook and so on. Each company on the lower establishment was commanded by a captain with two subalterns, and had a colour-sergeant, four sergeants, two drummers and about 100 rank and file (corporals and privates). The pioneers, transport drivers and bandsmen were borne on the strength of the companies, but when withdrawn to perform their particular duties the rank and file strength of a company was reduced to 93. In action the

Zulu shield, assegais and knobkerrie.

Zulus in full regalia. This photograph was taken in 1905, but their appearance would have been similar in 1879.

bandsmen usually served as stretcher bearers to the companies. Inevitably a battalion's actual strength in the field was less than the establishment, owing to casualties, sickness and men detached for other duties.

The battalion was armed with the Martini-Henry rifle and bayonet which was carried by every man except officers and staff sergeants. The Martini-Henry, which had been introduced into the Army in 1871, was a breech-loading, single-shot weapon with the breech operated by a lever fitted behind the trigger guard. Between eight and twelve aimed and up to twenty-five unaimed shots could be got off in a minute. It was sighted up to 1,450 yards. It fired a ·45-inch calibre brass cartridge containing a lead bullet weighing 480 grains, which by 1879 had already proved its effectiveness in stopping the onrush of savage enemies in the Second Afghan and the Ninth Kaffir Wars. The rifle weighed 9 lb, was 4 ft 1½ in long and, though accurate in skilled hands, it had a vicious recoil which caused young and inexperienced soldiers to flinch in anticipation, thus spoiling their aim. Dirt in the mechanism made it liable to jam, an unnerving experience if this occurred when a mass of screaming savages was bearing down on the firer. It also overheated badly after prolonged usage so that the barrel, despite its wooden stock, became too hot to hold. This defect had been discovered in the Ninth Kaffir War, and soldiers who had fought in that campaign had fitted their stocks with protective bullock-hide covers. The bayonet carried by the rank and file was of the socket type, with a 21½-inch blade of triangular section, whereas sergeants had a sword bayonet of similar length with a curved blade. This was the longest bayonet ever carried by the British infantry, but its extra 4½ inches of length over the model fitted to the previous rifle, the Snider, compensated for the loss of inches in the shorter Martini-Henry; an over-all reach of about 6 feet was deemed necessary for an infantryman,

British infantryman in undress uniform: glengarry cap and scarlet serge frock.

particularly when facing savage enemies. The infantry officer's regulation weapon was his sword, this still being of the Gothic-hilted 1822 pattern with brass guard but with the $32\frac{1}{2}$-inch, fullered blade introduced in 1845, carried in a steel scabbard. To supplement this elegant but somewhat useless weapon, officers would equip themselves with revolvers, the most popular types being the Webley and the Adams. During the Kaffir Wars earlier in the century many officers had acquired double-barrelled carbines, which proved very handy for bush fighting, but this practice seems to have lapsed by the time of the Zulu War.

Although clothing of a neutral shade had been adopted by some regiments in the Eighth Kaffir War of 1851–53, followed by the widespread use of khaki during the Sepoy Mutiny of 1857–58, which, when the Zulu War began, was also being worn by the troops in Afghanistan, the Army in Africa in the late 1870s still went to war in its home service clothing in the traditional colours. Although the full dress tunics, scarlet for infantry and engineers and blue for artillery, were discarded in favour of the easier-fitting undress serge frocks, these were still of the same colour, and were embellished with brass buttons and the different coloured facings of each regiment. The dark blue serge trousers with red stripes were tucked into black leather leggings. Officers wore their version of the serge frock or their dark blue patrol jackets, the latter being particularly favoured by officers on the staff. The only concession to foreign service for all ranks was the tropical helmet, worn without the puggarees used in India, and from which the brass spikes and regimental star plates had been removed. The white canvas covers were usually dyed brown with 'cow dung, ant-bear heap and coffee grounds'; tea was also used as a dye, or simply the reddish-brown mud found in that part of Africa. The regiments that had been through the Ninth Kaffir War probably had a fairly ragged appearance, as can be seen in a sketch by an officer of the 24th of two soldiers, one with a

21

British infantryman in full field service marching order. In South Africa the blue spiked helmet was replaced by the white foreign service pattern and the valise was usually carried on transport.

badly dented helmet, the other in a broad-brimmed hat, with patched frocks and trousers, one pair of which seems to be of canvas. A Lieutenant Knight of the Buffs recorded that 'out here our men fight in their shirt sleeves', but this was probably only when holding a fixed position.

The infantryman's accoutrements were of a relatively new design, the Valise Pattern Equipment, first introduced in 1871. This replaced the old knapsack and large black ammunition pouch suspended from a shoulder belt, which had been used in various forms since the previous century. Instead of the knapsack worn on the shoulders, the soldier had a waterproof valise of black canvas worn at the small of the back and supported over the shoulders by buff leather braces which divided into three on each side in front, two ends returning to top and bottom of the valise, the third being fastened to the buff waistbelt in front either side of the belt clasp. The ammunition was now carried in two buff leather pouches (black in some regiments), each containing twenty rounds, fitted to the belt either side of the clasp, with an additional black leather expense pouch, or ball bag, holding a further thirty rounds. The latter hung below the right-hand pouch or occasionally from the back of the waistbelt when the valise was not worn. On top of the valise, and below the greatcoat, which was folded and secured to the braces across the shoulders, was the semi-circular mess-tin in a black cover. The accoutrements were completed by the bayonet frog at the left hip, hanging under a white canvas haversack suspended over the right shoulder, and a barrel-shaped water bottle, capacity one quart, slung over the left. In South Africa the valises were normally carried on the regimental transport. These accoutrements had their disadvantages, but they were the first attempt to provide the soldiers with a properly balanced and integrated equipment. Furthermore the whole assembly could be stripped down to a lighter scale, and in some actions regiments fought in no more than

their belts, pouches, haversacks and water bottles. To support their swords and revolvers, officers wore either the regulation white leather waistbelt with slings, or variations on the Sam Browne belt, which had become popular in India after its invention by the Indian Cavalry officer of that name. To their belts they added haversacks, water bottles, binocular cases and ammunition pouches according to personal choice.

In the 1870 edition of *Field Exercises and Evolutions of Infantry*, the manual which governed the handling of an infantry battalion in the field, tactics had still been based on the close order of line, column and square of the Napoleonic and Crimean Wars, in which the basic sub-unit was the company formed in double rank. A battalion's fire was delivered in one of two ways: volleys, either by the whole battalion, half-battalions, companies, half-companies or sections, or independent fire, but the latter was only permitted 'under very exceptional circumstances'. Extended order was used for skirmishing during an advance to contact or protection of the main lines and columns, both in attack and defence. On such occasions a battalion would divide into skirmishers, supports and reserves, each group being of a given number of companies depending on the circumstances. In actual contact with the enemy's main body, close order would be adhered to. Owing, however, to the greatly increased range and rate of fire of the breech-loading rifle, the 1877 edition of the manual broke away for the first time from the time-honoured evolutions of line and column for field tactics, the new manoeuvres being based on the formations hitherto used for skirmishing, with much greater emphasis placed on the use of extended order. Instead of advancing to the attack with all its companies in line, a battalion would now close on the enemy with two companies extended as a firing line, another two in support ready to thicken up the firing line or protect its flanks, and the remaining four held back in reserve until required to reinforce the

Boy drummer in review order. The tunic is of the 1881 pattern, with round cuffs replacing the type shown in the previous photograph.

leading companies in the final charge on the enemy position. In defence a battalion was deployed in three similar groups. Whereas formerly great attention had been paid to the precision and accuracy required to maintain the close formation of line and column, these were now relegated to the barrack square. In the field, battalion commanders were urged to 'preserve elasticity of movement and advantage of the ground'.

Thus, on the outbreak of the Zulu War, infantry tactics were undergoing a radical transformation; but, as Viscount Wolseley pointed out in his *Soldier's Pocket Book*, extended order was only appropriate against an enemy armed with modern weapons, and 'in wars against barbarous nations the more you can with safety adopt a line or other close formation without unduly decreasing the effect of your breech-loading fire, the more advantage will your discipline give you over your undisciplined, though possibly more warlike enemy'. The danger of adopting an extended deployment against the onrush of the Zulus' charging buffalo formation was soon to be revealed in the opening stages of the war, and thereafter the troops were told that 'the enemy was to be treated as cavalry', to meet which they should 'adhere strictly to solid formations such as square'.

Before turning to the supporting arms and other elements of Chelmsford's army, another branch of the infantry must be noticed. It had long been the practice in South African campaigns to improvise detachments of mounted infantry drawn from the regular battalions to increase the mobility of field forces which were always short of regular cavalry. The 1/24th had raised and trained such a unit in 1875, of which the then G.O.C. at the Cape, Sir Arthur Cunynghame, said: 'The experiment created some amusement but my experience has always shown me that picked officers and men from foot regiments can in a very short time be turned into mounted riflemen of the very best description.' This troop, and another raised by the 88th, had served in the Ninth Kaffir War, and in 1878 the 1st and 2nd Squadrons, Imperial Mounted Infantry, were formed. Each was 150 strong, divided into two troops and drawn from the 2/3rd, 1/13th, 1/24th and 80th Regiments. The men were dressed and armed in normal infantry fashion but had bandoliers instead of ammunition pouches. Both were at Chelmsford's disposal in 1879.

The artillery available at the outset of the war consisted of N. Battery, 5th Brigade, Royal Field Artillery, and 11th Battery, 7th Brigade, Royal Garrison Artillery. To these would be added such guns as could be provided for land operations by the Royal Navy. Further batteries came out later in the campaign. A battery was commanded by a major, with 1

Infantry officer in campaign dress, Zululand: Major Campbell, 94th Regiment.

A fully accoutred mounted infantryman in South Africa.

captain, 3 lieutenants, a surgeon and a veterinary surgeon; 8 staff sergeants and sergeants; and 159 men, of which 72 were gunners, 64 drivers, and the remainder junior N.C.O.s, trumpeters and artificers. The horses numbered 30 for riding and 102 for draught. A battery was organized into three sections, each manning two guns, which in South Africa were of the type known as 7-pounder Rifled Muzzle Loading (R.M.L.). It could fire shrapnel, common shell, double shell or case-shot, and had a range of 3,100 yards. One of the later batteries to arrive and another detachment of the Royal Navy were equipped with the 9-pounder R.M.L. which, though firing a heavier projectile, had slightly less range than the 7-pounder. Some breech-loading guns had been introduced in the 1860s, but, after trials had disclosed no great improvement in performance over the simpler and less expensive muzzle-loaders, the latter had been readopted. In addition to guns the Royal

An officer, N.C.O.s and men of a Royal Artillery battery in Zululand with two 7-pounder R.M.L. field guns.

Officers, N.C.O.s and men of the Royal Engineers.

Artillery batteries and the Naval Brigade had a number of Hale's rockets, the 9-pounder type used by the Army and the 24-pounder of the Navy. The rocket had either an explosive or incendiary warhead, had an effective range of about 1,300 yards, and emitted in flight a high-pitched shriek which could well have an alarming effect on unsophisticated opponents. Their accuracy left much to be desired but they were reasonably effective against a mass target. The 9-pounder rockets were fired from a V-shaped iron trough mounted on a tripod, but the Navy used a tube for their 24-pounders. An extra battery of three 9-pounder rocket troughs was formed under Major Russell, R.A., and manned by men of the 24th Regiment trained in their use. The third weapon to be used in the campaign, first only by the Royal Navy but later also by the Royal Artillery, was the Gatling Gun. The Gatling consisted of ten rifled barrels revolving round a central shaft, fed from a cylindrical magazine, and fired by rotating a crank handle. It was mounted on a carriage similar to that of a field gun. It fired a ·45-inch calibre round, was effective up to 1,200 yards, had a rate of fire up to 400 rounds per minute but was prone to jamming.

The Royal Artillery's full dress tunic was dark blue with red facings, but in the field officers usually wore a blue patrol jacket, similar to those of infantry officers, while the men appeared in serge frocks. The gunners, but not drivers, of a battery were armed with sword bayonets for their personal protection and additionally two Snider carbines were issued to each gun detachment.

Two field companies of Royal Engineers were available to Chelmsford. At war strength a field company was commanded by a major, with 5 other officers, 21 N.C.O.s, 175 men, 15 riding horses and 31 draught, and 6 store wagons. Since both companies sent out to South Africa, however, were only commanded by captains, they must have been at reduced strength. Sappers were dressed, armed and accoutred similarly to infantry and were capable of acting as such if the occasion demanded and if they could be spared from engineering duties. At the outset of the campaign only one company and the advance party of the other had reached the force in the field; the balance was still marching up from Durban.

No regiments of regular cavalry were in South Africa in early 1879 but since two – the 1st King's Dragoon Guards and 17th Lancers – were sent out from England for the latter part of the war they may as well be considered here. A cavalry regiment at the war establishment had 31 officers, 43 staff sergeants and sergeants, 22 artificers (farriers, saddlers, smiths, etc.) and 549 rank and file, of which 15 were bandsmen

Captain's tunic, 1st King's Dragoon Guards.

and 22 transport drivers, and 615 horses. The total all ranks should have been 653, but the King's Dragoon Guards embarked with 634 and the 17th with 622. The regiment was organized into a headquarters, of similar composition to that of the infantry battalion but with a veterinary surgeon instead of the second major, and eight troops, two of which formed a squadron. A troop had three officers, a troop-sergeant-major, three sergeants, four corporals, two artificers, a trumpeter, sixty privates and a driver.

With regard to armament, officers of heavy and light cavalry had different pattern swords to which they probably added a revolver when on service. Troopers of all types of cavalry carried the same sword, of the 1864 pattern with pierced sheet steel guard, 35-inch long blade and carried in a steel scabbard, together with a Martini-Henry carbine. In addition the lancer had his 1868 pattern lance, made of a 9-foot bamboo shaft with a steel point and butt and

Sailors and Marines (in centre) of the naval Brigade from H.M.S. Active, *with a 12-pounder Armstrong (Sea Service) gun on the left and a Gatling gun on the right.*

The Durban Mounted Rifles parading for active service, 1879. Their uniform was dark blue with black facings, piped scarlet, and a scarlet stripe down the breeches.

Scouts of the Frontier Light Horse. Their uniform was buff corduroy with black trimmings. Black or blue patrol jackets were worn by officers and senior N.C.O.s. An engraving from the Illustrated London News *after a sketch by Captain Lawrence, 4th King's Own.*

red-over-white pennon. Staff sergeants, troop-sergeant-majors and trumpeters were armed with sword and revolver.

The K.D.G.s wore scarlet tunics, with blue facings, and dark blue breeches with a $1\frac{3}{4}$-inch yellow stripe (gold for officers). The 17th had blue double-breasted tunics, faced white, with a plastron front which in full dress showed white, but on service was buttoned over to show blue, and a red and yellow waist girdle; their breeches were blue with a double white stripe. Both regiments wore knee boots and the foreign service helmet. The cavalryman's accoutrements consisted of a waistbelt with slings to suspend the sword, which in the 17th was worn under the tunic, and a buff leather pouch belt, suspending the black leather pouch

containing thirty rounds of ammunition. In the field, troopers were issued with a haversack and water bottle of the infantry pattern, which were both slung over the right shoulder.

The contribution of the Royal Navy to the land forces consisted of detachments of officers and seamen, Royal Marine Artillery and Royal Marine Light Infantry from H.M. Ships *Active, Boadicea, Euphrates, Forester, Himalaya, Orontes, Shah, Tamar* and *Tenedos.* They served as infantry and as gunners, manning the types of guns mentioned earlier. At the start of operations the Naval Brigade only mustered some 200 men, but the total later rose to just over 800. In the field, naval officers wore either their peaked caps or the foreign service helmet, with double- or single-breasted blue frocks and white or blue trousers, while the seamen wore the sennet straw hat or their flat caps, and white or blue jumpers and trousers with canvas leggings. Sailors when ashore had brown leather accoutrements. The dress and equipment of the Royal Marine Artillery and Light Infantry followed that of the Royal Artillery and the Infantry.

Such were the regular troops available to Chelmsford in January 1879. Excluding the two cavalry regiments, they totalled some 5,400 all ranks at hand for active operations; a number of infantry companies had to be detached to man static garrisons on the lines of communication, while some battalions, like the 1/24th, had companies in other parts of southern Africa. With the exception of the recently arrived 2/4th, 99th and the R.E. companies, the other battalions and batteries had been in the country for a year or more and had seen active service in the Ninth Kaffir War and Sekukuni's rebellion. In the wake of the Crimean War twenty-four years earlier many reforms had been made in the Army, particularly in building up the administrative services which had been virtually non-existent before the Crimea: the Army Medical Staff, Army Hospital Corps, Commissariat and Transport Department, Army Service Corps, Ordnance Store Branch and Corps, elements of which supported Chelmsford's army in the field.

Further reforms, to conditions of service and recruitment, had followed the appointment of Edward Cardwell as Secretary of State for War in 1868. Notable among these had been, first, the abolition in 1871 of the long-standing purchase system by which officers bought their commissions and promotion (up to the rank of lieutenant-colonel). Henceforth commissioning would be by competitive examination, followed by training as a gentleman cadet at Sandhurst for cavalry and infantry and at Woolwich for artillery and engineers. Thereafter promotion was to be by seniority, theoretically tempered by selection. Nevertheless, there were among

Officers of the Durban Mounted Rifles. Standing: R. Jameson, D. Buchanan. Seated: W. Shepstone and T. Shepstone. On ground: D. Moodie.

the officers of Chelmsford's army many who had been commissioned under the old system. The new arrangement made little change to the social backgrounds of officers, who continued to be drawn from the upper and upper middle classes, largely because the rising Victorian middle class had no tradition of, or even desire for, military service.

Cardwell's second great reform affected the non-commissioned ranks: he abolished the old system of long service, under which a man enlisted for a minimum of ten years with the colours, after which most re-engaged for a further eleven. In its place came a twelve-year engagement, of which six were to be served with the colours and six with the reserve. The purpose was to build up the reserves, of which hitherto there had been none, so that the Army could be rapidly expanded in time of war, and also to attract a better type of man into the ranks. At the same time he aimed to equalize the number of battalions between home and foreign stations, so that a battalion at home could recruit and train drafts for its counterpart abroad. For regiments with two battalions this posed no problem, but the single-battalion regiments had to be linked in pairs for this purpose, though retaining their own identity. This system was introduced in 1872, but the fact that both battalions of the 24th were in South Africa showed that it was not working correctly. Cardwell's proposals for short service, too, had met with much opposition, many officers maintaining that regiments comprised mainly of young soldiers would lack the steadiness, robust qualities and experience of battalions composed of long-service soldiers. In 1879 there were in fact numbers of the latter still in the ranks, particularly in a battalion like the 1/24th which had been overseas since 1866, and even the younger men of the 2/24th had grown in maturity since their experience in the Ninth Kaffir War. The same applied to the 1/13th who in 1877 had had a high proportion of what were little more than recruits. The early reverses of the Zulu War were to be attributed in part to the defects of short service by its opponents, but they failed to notice that the chief victims came from a battalion of which about half were long-service men.

The second element of Chelmsford's army, the Colonial irregulars, presented a multiplicity of small bodies, ranging from those like the Natal Hussars and Buffalo Border Guard, each about 30 strong, to the Frontier Light Horse and Baker's Horse which, mustering over 200 men each, represented the strongest European volunteer units in the force. The importance of these volunteers was that, apart from the Imperial Mounted Infantry, they were the only mounted troops that Chelmsford possessed in January 1879, and as such were vital for reconnaissance, protection and escorts. Apart from the 110-strong Natal Mounted Police, who were enlisted like regular soldiers, many of them direct from England, the local forces were all part-timers, called out only when the need

arose and for the occasional drill. They were a mixture of the Boer commando system, which laid a military obligation on every adult male, and the Volunteer Movement of 1859 in England. All male colonists in Natal had an obligation to serve, but, being mainly of English extraction, they did not adapt easily to the rough and ready practicality of the Boer system, and if they had to soldier would only do so, as had the Volunteers in England, in a more structured organization with uniforms, ranks and units with exotic names. Furthermore, while many colonists volunteered out of a sense of duty, there were others, again like the Volunteers, who were more attracted by the pseudo-dignity of a uniform and military rank than by the needs of training and discipline.

All this, together with a lack of centralized control over the local forces, resulted in a proliferation of small, under-strength units of doubtful military value, with some members quick to find reasons for their absence when the bugle sounded the call to arms. Thus, in the 1,000-odd mounted volunteers Chelmsford was able to muster for the war, no fewer than fifteen units including the Mounted Police were represented. On the other hand, many of those that did turn out were excellent material: skilled horsemen, good shots, knowledgeable about the country and used to an open-air life. Some of the units, like the Frontier Light Horse under a British officer, Major Redvers Buller of the 60th Rifles, had the advantage of coming straight from the Kaffir War or Sekukuni's rebellion, and were thus experienced and accustomed to working together. In an attempt to acquire some of the finest mounted infantry in Africa for the campaign, overtures had been made to the Transvaal Boers, who had no love for the Zulus, but of all the Boers only one man, Piet Uys, came forward with his four sons and forty burghers, giving their services without wish for reward.

The arms and accoutrements of the colonial troops consisted usually of a rifle or carbine and a bandolier. The firearms were either of the

Snider and Martini-Henry type or a variation of the latter, the Swinburne-Henry. Although some units had full dress uniforms whose splendour rivalled that of the regulars, in the field jackets and breeches of black, brown or buff corduroy were most customary, worn with slouch hats or forage caps, while some had foreign service helmets and black or blue patrol jackets or frocks.

Although Chelmsford's forces obviously enjoyed a superiority of firepower, this was to some extent offset by the much greater mobility of a Zulu army, and the European force he could put into the field was outnumbered by about seven to one. Furthermore the possibility of an impi slipping across almost anywhere along the 200-mile frontier into Natal or the Transvaal required the provision of guards and garrisons for vital points, supply depots and lines of communication before a campaign began, and would increasingly weaken his field force as it progressed; hence the decision mentioned earlier to raise further troops from the only possible remaining source, the Natal Kaffirs.

Seven thousand of these men were conscripted to form three infantry regiments of the Natal Native Contingent, as it was called, the 1st Regiment having three battalions, the others only two. A battalion had ten companies, each of nine European officers and N.C.O.s and 100 natives. The force was beset with difficulties from the start. Instead of being issued with uniforms, they had to be content with a red rag tied round their heads. Only enough firearms could be found to arm one man in ten, and many of these were of an obsolete pattern; the remainder had to make do with the same weapons as the enemy. Although most, if not all, the battalion commanders were adequate regular or colonial officers, to find the 300-odd European officers and N.C.O.s to train and lead these levies – all of whom were straight off their kraals with no knowledge or experience of European drill and tactics – the barrel of white manpower had to be scraped, for the best colonials were already serving in the mounted units. The results, on the whole, were unhappy. Many of the N.C.O.s were very rough diamonds, with no more knowledge of drill or weapon training than their unfortunate men, whom they bullied with a cruel contempt. Only in the 1st Regiment, under Lieutenant-Colonel Durnford, Royal Engineers, who had a

European officers and Kaffirs of the Natal Native Contingent.

33

Men of Major Bengough's 2/1st Regiment, Natal Native Contingent. They have no uniforms except a red rag tied round their foreheads.

sympathetic understanding of the Kaffirs and who managed to obtain European subordinates of a better calibre, was any progress made with turning the raw material into a force of some military value.

Of a more encouraging nature were the 6 troops of some 200 mounted Kaffirs known as the Natal Native Horse, all uniformed, well mounted and armed with carbines, and two companies of Natal Native Pioneers, armed and equipped with picks and shovels, who would make good the dearth of sappers caused by the delayed arrival on the border of one of the R.E. companies. The native troops were completed by two battalions of friendly Zulus.

With the addition of 9,000 native levies to the regulars and colonials, and including the garrisons earmarked for Natal and the Transvaal, Chelmsford mustered a fighting force of about 16,000 men. Much of it lacked

training and equipment, some of it was of very doubtful quality, but it had a solid backbone in the regular battalions, and it was the best that could be assembled between the time he was ordered by Frere to consider the possibility of military action against Zululand and the expiry of the ultimatum to Cetshwayo.

If the assembly of adequate forces had stretched the manpower and armoury of the colony to the limit, the problems of supplying and maintaining such an army with food, water, fuel, ammunition, tentage, equipment, and above all transportation for these commodities, presented equal, if not greater, difficulties. Reckoning on operations lasting between six weeks and two months, Chelmsford calculated that 1,800 tons of stores would be needed to accompany the army. The most common form of transport in South Africa was the ox wagon, 18 feet long and 6 feet wide, which required

Basutos of the type that formed a troop of the Natal Native Horse.

between fourteen and eighteen beasts to draw it. To keep the oxen in good working trim, sixteen hours a day had to be allowed for their grazing and rest, so that on the rough dirt tracks only about 10 miles a day could be covered, even under good conditions. If the way was strewn with boulders, seamed with water courses or churned up by the rains, this could be reduced to three or four. Not only would the rate of advance be limited by these slow-moving vehicles and the herds of slaughter cattle required for the meat ration, but they also offered a huge and highly vulnerable target to the fast-moving Zulus and would therefore need further detachments from the striking force to protect them.

The amassing of baggage and draught animals with their vehicles in sufficient quantities from the relatively scanty resources of Natal proved a time-consuming and increasingly expensive business for Chelmsford and his staff but, by scouring the colony, the Transvaal and even the Cape, and by paying greatly inflated prices, by January 1879 there had been collected 977 wagons, 56 carts, 10,023 oxen, 803 horses and 398 mules, with 2,000 extra natives to drive and manage them.

So, as Frere's ultimatum was presented to Cetshwayo's inDunas, the two widely differing armies stood ready. On the one hand, there was the great Zulu host of eager warriors impatient to wash their spears, lightly-equipped, rapid-moving, but armed only with primitive weapons. On the other, there was Chelmsford's field force, numerically inferior and with more than half of it untested and of dubious value, encumbered with a vast and unwieldy logistic train, but with its best elements armed with the most modern firearms. Even if the whole force could be concentrated against the Zulu Army, the result would not be a foregone conclusion. As it was, when Chelmsford came to plan his operation, he decided it would be necessary to divide his forces.

3

The Plans

Zululand is a country of rolling green downlands and red earth, studded with prominent, rocky-topped hills and seamed with twisting water courses. Although the countryside has an open aspect, the grasslands can prove rough going, broken by boulders, ant-bear heaps, thorn scrub and gullies. In 1879 there were no roads and only a series of native tracks running between the kraals with their beehive huts. From a low-lying coastal strip the land rises gradually to the west, where among the higher hills streams flow back eastwards to form the Black and White Umfolozi Rivers, running laterally across the country to meet some 30 miles from the coast, and entering the sea just south of St Lucia Bay. About 20 miles further south the Umhlatuzi River flows roughly parallel with the Umfolozi. Between the Umhlatuzi and the Natal border along the Tugela, three shorter rivers, the Umlalazi, Inyezane and Amatikulu, run parallel with each other towards the Indian Ocean.

From the coast just north of the Natal town of Stanger, the border followed the meandering course of the Tugela in a roughly westerly direction for some 90 miles, or 60 as the crow flies, until it turned north-west up the Buffalo River, reaching the southernmost tip of the territory disputed between the Boers and the Zulus at Rorke's Drift, another twisting 40 miles upstream. About 10 miles further on, where the Blood River flows into the Buffalo,

the course of the former marked the western boundary of the disputed territory and therefore, after the findings of the Boundary Commission, the revised Transvaal-Zululand border, while the Buffalo to the west divided the Transvaal from Natal. At a point about 40 miles up the Blood River, 10 miles east of Utrecht, the Zulu border turned north-east until it reached the Pongola River 50 miles east of Luneburg in the Transvaal.

The main points of entry into Zululand from Natal were three: at the Lower Tugela Drift near the coast where the road from Durban and Stanger met a track on the Zulu bank which led to Eshowe and thence, via a mission station at St Paul's, to the royal kraal at Ulundi; at the Middle Tugela Drift, reached from the Pietermaritzburg–Greytown road and from which another track ran to Eshowe; and from Helpmakaar to Rorke's Drift where a track ran to Ulundi via Ibabanango. Thus there were adequate communications within Natal towards the border from Pietermaritzburg and Durban, and, since Helpmakaar was linked by road to Greytown, from which a narrow track ran to the Lower Tugela Drift, there was also a lateral route parallel with the border, roughly 10 miles south of the Tugela. Wagons could be driven across the drifts in the dry season, but during the January rains they had to be ferried across on flat-bottomed, iron ponts. In the north Zululand could be entered from the Transvaal

Top Left: Colonel Charles Knight Pearson, 3rd Buffs, commanding No. 1 or Right Column. The uniform is that of c. 1856 and shows Pearson as a lieutenant.

Top Right: Colonel Richard Glyn, 24th Regiment, commanding No. 3, or Centre Column. Water colour by Lt-Col. J. N. Crealock, Chelmsford's Military Secretary.

Bottom Left: Colonel Evelyn Wood, V.C., 90th Light infantry, commanding No. 4 or Left Column.

by a track running east from Utrecht which crossed the Blood River at a difficult drift near a hill called Bemba's Kop.

When Chelmsford began to assess the military problem in August 1878, it did not take him long to realize that the border of some 200 miles, which the highly mobile Zulus, unfettered by transport, could cross at any number of places, was indefensible with the number of troops at his command. If, as Frere believed, the Zulus really posed a threat to Natal and the Transvaal, the colonies could only be protected by invading Zululand to bring the Zulu Army to battle, defeating it in the field and capturing the royal kraal at Ulundi. This was easier said than done. To offset his numerical inferiority, the ideal solution would be to concentrate his available troops into one strong striking force and drive for Ulundi. Such a course, however, could not guarantee his being able to locate the Zulu Army, which might simply bypass his slow-moving column and thrust behind him into a defenceless Natal. Furthermore an invasion would have to be timed to take place before the grass on which his oxen and horses would depend for grazing dried out; an advance after April might be met by a blazing inferno as the Zulus set the veldt aflame. On the other hand, the primitive tracks in the rainy season would quickly be churned into an impassable sea of mud if only a single axis of advance was used, and the time one long, cumbersome column would take to cross the flooded rivers would leave his force highly vulnerable. Everything pointed, therefore, to an early invasion, using a number of different axes for a concentric advance on Ulundi. Such a course would weaken his greatest asset, the firepower of his guns and infantry, and would lessen the time available for preparation, training the non-regular elements of his force, and acclimatizing and toughening up the most recently arrived troops from England. Moreover, the Zulus, with the advantage of interior lines, mobility and numbers, could strike with overwhelming strength against any one part of the invading

army. Against these drawbacks could be set the speedier rate of advance and reduced strain on the routes and logistic resources that would be achieved by smaller columns, while their separate advance into Zululand must inevitably draw the enemy's attention, alarm Cetshwayo into giving battle, and deter him from any counter-thrust into Natal. Beyond that the outcome would depend on the power of the ·45 bullet to drop the warrior before he got within stabbing range with his assegai.

Ulundi lay in the centre of Zululand just north of the White Umfolozi and approximately 70 miles equidistant from any part of the frontier. None of the approaches, therefore, had more to commend it than any other as far as distance was concerned. All would have to cross one or more of the lateral rivers within Zululand, and, although an advance from the Lower Tugela Drift would also have to negotiate the three small rivers between the Umhlatuzi and the Tugela, it offered a shorter and better route to Eshowe than that from the Middle Drift, which, though bypassing the small rivers, passed through some very broken country. Chelmsford therefore determined to use the routes through the Lower Drift, Rorke's Drift and the northernmost one by Bemba's Kop with a mixed column of all arms on each. He also decided to position a smaller force at the Middle Drift in an attempt to convince the Zulus that a fourth advance was intended from that place, to deny any use of the drift by the enemy, and to act as a reserve. A fifth column was to be held in readiness at Luneburg in the Transvaal as a further reserve, and to keep a watchful eye both on the Boers and on the northern border of Zululand.

Since the two outer start points of the three main columns would be 70 and 35 miles apart as the crow flies from the centre, each column would have to act independently and be entirely self-supporting. Not until the columns began to converge on Ulundi would Chelmsford be able to exercise command over the army as a whole. In the meantime he elected to move with his staff on the central route from Rorke's Drift. Command of the centre column itself was in the hands of Colonel Glyn of the 24th Regiment, a short, rather irascible officer lately in command of the 1st Battalion, whose performance in the Kaffir War had earned him Bartle Frere's commendation as 'an excellent, steady and sensible commander'. Colonel Pearson of the 3rd Buffs, a methodical and prudent veteran of the Crimean War, was given the right column, and Colonel Evelyn Wood the left. Though lately in command of the 90th Light Infantry, Wood had served as a midshipman of the Royal Navy in the Crimea, had transferred to the Army and won the Victoria Cross with the 17th Lancers in the Sepoy Mutiny. More recently he had done good work in command of a regiment of native levies in Wolseley's successful Ashanti Campaign of 1873. He was susceptible to all manner of illnesses and was highly accident-prone, but he had an unquenchable courage and spirit, and was a thoroughly hard-working, progressive and competent professional soldier. The force at Middle Drift, which was largely to consist of native levies, was put under the aforementioned Lieutenant-Colonel Durnford, R.E., and the Transvaal column under Colonel Rowlands, another holder of the Victoria Cross who had won it with the 41st Regiment in the Crimea.

After various detachments had been made for garrisoning the entry points, the remaining regulars were divided more or less equally between the three main columns; each column had its share of artillery and mounted troops. The newly-arrived 2/4th King's Own was deprived of the chance to take part in the invasion, since four of its companies were left to garrison Utrecht while the other four took over protection of the lines of communication from three of the 1/24th. One company of the 1/24th was on detached duty in Pondoland, and, although the other three were all relieved by the 2/4th by 10 January, and were marching up to join their battalion, they would not reach the border before the ultimatum expired. At Rorke's Drift the crossing place was guarded by B Company of the 2/24th, under its commander, Lieutenant Bromhead, who at thirty-three was somewhat elderly for a subaltern and whose increasing deafness may have contributed to his selection for this necessary but less taxing post. The crossing at the Lower Drift was protected on the south bank by a fort named after the column commander and manned by a company of sailors and some of the N.N.C.; a further fort, Tenedos, was to be constructed on the Zulu bank manned by another naval company from the ship of that name and two companies of the 99th.

The field force was formed as follows.

No. 1 Column. Colonel Pearson. Lower Drift
Naval Brigade (including Royal Marines) with two 7-pounders, two 24-pounder rocket tubes, one Gatling.

One section, 11th Battery, 7th Brigade, Royal Garrison Artillery (two 7-pounders, one rocket trough).

2nd Field Company, Royal Engineers.

2nd Battalion, 3rd Regiment (The Buffs).

99th Regiment, less two companies.

One troop, Imperial Mounted Infantry (24th).

Five troops, Colonial Mounted Volunteers (Natal Hussars; Durban, Alexandra, Stanger and Victoria Mounted Rifles; each troop 40–50 strong).

2nd Regiment, Natal Native Contingent (two battalions).

One company, Natal Native Pioneers.

No. 2 Column. Lieutenant-Colonel Durnford, Middle Drift
One rocket battery (three 9-pounders; Major and bombardier R.A., eight men 1/24th).

1st Regiment, Natal Native Contingent (three battalions).

Six troops, Natal Native Horse.

No. 3 Column. Colonel Glyn. Rorke's Drift
N Battery, 5th Brigade, Royal Field Artillery (six 7-pounders, two rocket troughs).

Advance Party, 5th Field Company, Royal Engineers.

1st Battalion, 24th Regiment, less four companies (three *en route*).

2nd Battalion, 24th Regiment, less one company.

One squadron, Imperial Mounted Infantry (2/3rd, 1/13th, 1/24th, 80th).

One squadron, Natal Mounted Police.

One squadron, Colonial Mounted Volunteers (Natal Carbineers, Newcastle Mounted Rifles, Buffalo Border Guard).

3rd Regiment, Natal Native Contingent (two battalions).

One company, Natal Native Pioneers.

No. 4 Column. Colonel Wood. Bemba's Kop

11th Battery, 7th Brigade, Royal Garrison Artillery, less one section (four 7-pounders, two rocket troughs).

1st Battalion, 13th Light Infantry.

90th Light Infantry.

Six troops, Colonial Mounted Volunteers (Frontier Light Horse (4), Baker's Horse (2)).

One troop, Boer Burghers.

Two battalions, Wood's Irregulars (friendly Zulus).

No. 5 Column. Colonel Rowlands. Luneburg

80th Regiment (also manning two 6-pounders and one 4-pounder).

Cape Mounted Riflemen (Colonial). (Formerly Frontier Armed and Mounted Police.)

Colonial Mounted Volunteers (Border Horse, Ferreira's Horse, Schutte's Corps).

Eckersley's Transvaal Native Contingent.

At Luneburg, but not part of column: one troop, Kaffrarian Vanguard (Germans).

Each column was instructed that the main aim of the invasion was the destruction of the Zulu Army and the capture of Cetshwayo by a general advance on Ulundi, starting on 11 January. Pearson's No. 1 Column was given as its initial objective the establishment of an advanced base at Eshowe, from which he was to co-ordinate his further advance with Chelmsford and Glyn in the centre. Glyn's column was to head due east and establish a base near Isipezi Hill, 22 miles inside Zululand. Wood was given considerable latitude within the over-all aim for the operation of his column, which Chelmsford hoped would prevent the northern Zulus from interfering with the centre column. With regard to Durnford's column, Chelmsford was undecided. Since Durnford only had native troops and also a reputation for impulsiveness, Chelmsford was unwilling to grant him the latitude he was prepared to allow Wood. Furthermore he was worried about the vulnerability to a Zulu raid of Umsinga, half-way between Helpmakaar and Greytown on the important road leading up from Pietermaritzburg. At the same time he was not prepared to leave the Middle Drift unprotected. Ultimately he ordered that two battalions of the 1st N.N.C. should remain at Middle Drift, the third battalion to move to Umsinga, and that Durnford himself with the Rocket Battery and the Natal Native Horse should move up to join the centre column. Thus No. 2 Column was broken up and Durnford, much to his chagrin, deprived of an independent command.

The operation orders to the columns were backed up by a mass of regulations to be observed by the field force, which ranged from the treatment of natives to recipes for curried stew and toad-in-the-hole. Particular attention was paid to the selection, protection and hygiene of camp sites. Camps were to be set out so that troops could move quickly and without confusion to their alarm posts in the event of a night attack. They were to be 'partially entrenched on all sides', and covered by obstacles such as bushes forming a *chevaux de frise* and broken bottles stuck in the ground. If attacked, tents would be struck so as to give a clear field of fire in all directions. By day protection would be afforded by vedettes posted at some distance in good observation posts, and all grazing horses and oxen were to have mounted guards. At night the horses were to be picketed and the oxen placed in a laager, the whole camp guarded by outlying picquets of infantry on all sides, with ten-men parties of natives interspersed to give timely warning of any enemy approach. Chelmsford had been

Types of transport used by Chelmsford's field force, as drawn by Lieutenant C. Penrose, Royal Engineers:

GENERAL SERVICE WAGON

WEIGHT 18 CWT. TRACK 5'.2".

HEIGHT OF DRAUGHT. 2·8'

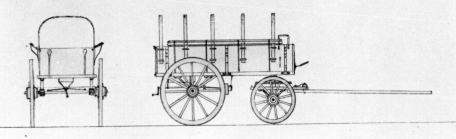

WHEELS

	Fore	Hind
Wt	1-0-12	1-0-24
Dish	$2\frac{1}{2}$ ins	$2\frac{1}{2}$ ins

Width of tire $2\frac{1}{2}$ ins

SCALE $\frac{1}{60}$

INCHES ... FEET.

COLONIAL OX WAGON (TENT).

Weight 29 cwt. Track 5'8'. 16 to 20 oxen.

Height of Draught. 2·3.

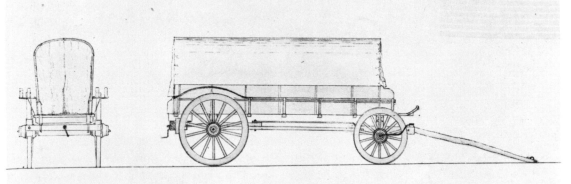

WHEELS

	Fore	Hind
Wt	1-1-0	1-2-0
Dish	2 ins	$3\frac{1}{2}$ ins

Width of tire 3 ins.

Scale $\frac{1}{60}$.

Inches ... Feet

41

COLONIAL MULE WAGON.

Weight 16 cwt. 8 to 10 mules.

Height of Draught 2·6.

WHEELS

	Fore	Hind
Wt	1 - 3 - 7	2 - 1 - 20
Dish	1/2 in	1/2 in
Width of tire	2½ ins	

Scale 1/60 .

Inches |12 0 1 2 3 4 5 6 7 8 9 10| Feet

AMBULANCE. M.III.

WEIGHT 18 CWT. TRACK 5·2

HEIGHT OF DRAUGHT 2·8

WHEELS.

	Fore	Hind
WT	0 - 3 - 12	1 - 1 - 0
Dish	2½ ins	2½ ins
Width of tire	2 ins	

ACCOMMODATION

2. STRETCHERS. 5 MEN SITTING.

A. CORN LOCKER
B. WATER-TANK
C. STORE-BOX
D. REST FOR WATER BARREL
E. BRAKE.
F. FILLING TUBE.

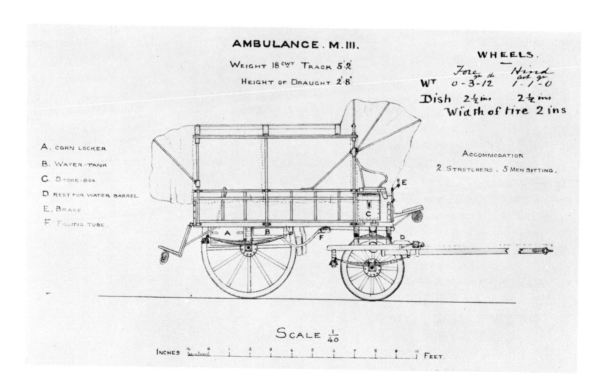

SCALE 1/40

INCHES |12 0 1 2 3 4 5 6 7 8 9 10| FEET.

impressed by the faith placed by the Boers in wagon laagers, and paragraph 20 of his regulations contained the following:

'Troops marching through the enemy's country, or where there is any possibility of attack, will, when halting, though but for a few hours, invariably form a wagon laager. The wagons should not only be locked together in laager formation but the defence should be further strengthened by the intervals between the outer wheels being built up with earth, stones, brushwood etc. The formation of a wagon laager is not to interfere with the construction of trenches, walls or other defences of the camp, but is intended to act as a citadel for the troops to retire into in the event of their being hard-pressed or outnumbered.'

Since victory would ultimately depend on firepower, considerable attention was paid in the regulations to ammunition. Each two-gun section of a battery carried 68 rounds and 12 rockets in a Scotch cart drawn by four mules, with a reserve of 100 rounds, 10 of double shell and 36 rockets in an ox wagon, giving 89 rounds per gun and 48 rockets. Small arms ammunition for infantry and mounted riflemen was scaled at 270 rounds per man, 70 on the soldier and 200 reserve carried in the company transport.

The regulations reminded all officers and N.C.O.s that:

'Too much care cannot be taken in restraining their men when in action from too lavish an expenditure of ammunition. Seventy rounds are carried by each soldier but these are quickly expended, if he is carried away by excitement, and does not fire with coolness and precision. There is obvious danger should men run short of ammunition when at any distance from the reserves. Whenever, therefore, there appears any likelihood of troops becoming hotly engaged, thirty rounds extra had better be carried by the soldier. A N. C. Officer should always be previously detailed by each company, whose duty it would be should an engagement become imminent to have the reserve ammunition in readiness for issue from the wagons.'

These strictures concluded with warnings about ensuring the means of transport for further reserves and stressed that 'a commanding officer would incur a heavy responsibility should required supplies fail to arrive in time, through any want of foresight and arrangement on his part'.

From such operational matters the regulations passed on to administrative requirements, like the men's health needing flannel rather than cotton shirts, the greasing of boots instead of blacking, and the ration scale. Of meat, each officer and man was entitled to $1\frac{1}{4}$ lb of fresh, 1 lb of salt or 1 lb of preserved; of bread, $1\frac{1}{2}$ lb of fresh or 1 lb of biscuit. Groceries and vegetables were included, though when these were not fresh each man was to receive 1 oz of lime juice with $\frac{1}{2}$ oz of sugar to make it palatable. The great standby of the old long-service soldier, his daily $\frac{1}{2}$ gill of rum, was not omitted, but before it was issued the senior medical officer was required to certify, in writing, that it was necessary. Chelmsford was not standing the risk of any drunkenness in the ranks. The native levies had to make do with meat and mealies. The scales of transport for each element of the force were carefully laid down with their respective loads, each company of infantry, for example, being allotted two wagons to carry its tents, tools, reserve ammunition, blankets (one per man), cooking equipment, rations, stretchers, heliograph for signalling, officers' baggage and men's valises. Mindful of the need for entrenching, each company's tools included fifteen each of picks, shovels, axes and billhooks. The total wagons for a battalion, therefore, numbered sixteen for the companies and one for battalion headquarters; a squadron of mounted infantry required three; and a battery of artillery had ten vehicles of different types.

Taking everything into consideration, Chelmsford had, in the time available, put a pretty well-found force into the field. The operational plan involved a number of risks, but when all the circumstances are balanced it is difficult to see that it could have been much improved. In the face of very considerable difficulties and obstructions, Chelmsford had done his best to ensure that the force would not founder, as many British armies had in the past, for want of logistic support. Finally, he had taken pains to inform all ranks about the nature and characteristics of the enemy they were about to face and what would be expected of them in the field. As he sat on his horse on the banks of the Buffalo in the early hours of 11 January 1879, he may have had some misgivings, but he also had cause to feel quietly confident about his arrangements.

At Ulundi, 70 miles away, Cetshwayo's preparations had been of a more simple character. Indeed, on that same morning, he had made very few. After he had first received from John Dunn the staggering demands of Frere's ultimatum, his Great Council had met but, apart from arranging for the summoning of the executioners of Sihayo's wife and the rounding-up of cattle with which to pay the fines, he had done nothing other than ask Frere for more time to get the malefactors and cattle to the border.

Since then, 18 December, he had been waiting for a reply that never came. He had no need to summon his regiments to Ulundi as a precautionary measure, for his army was already close at hand, having assembled for the traditional festival of the First Fruits, a time when new laws were made and the army was reviewed, accompanied by much celebration. Even when he learned that the columns mustering on the border had advanced, he still seemed reluctant to order his warriors to battle, hoping perhaps that the war he had not wanted might yet be avoided. Some of his older advisers counselled caution but the younger men, whose unmarried regiments were straining to show their mettle, were all for action. Had Cetshwayo been prepared to comply with all Frere's demands, it seems unlikely that he would have been able to restrain the lust for battle of his unblooded warriors. Nevertheless it was not

until 17 January that he decided to pick up the gauntlet thrown down by the British and send out his men to fight. The only strategic decision he appears to have made was not to commit the whole of his army. The main impi, over 20,000 strong, was despatched westwards towards Rorke's Drift; another totalling about 6,000 was sent south, and some of the older regiments were held back as a reserve. Cetshwayo did not accompany his troops, entrusting them to the joint command of the septuagenarian Tshingwayo and the forty-year-old Mavumengwana; his brother Dabulamanzi led the Undi corps. Twelve regiments formed the main impi, their age-groups ranging from the elderly umKhulutshane of men in their sixties to the early twenties of the 3,500-strong uVe, one of the only two regiments raised by Cetshwayo himself. Apart from giving the impi its general objective, his orders were simple in the extreme: they were to march slowly to conserve their strength and only to fight in daylight; the enemy could be recognized by their red coats; and on no account was the Natal border to be crossed. The five regiments sent south under Umatyiya were presumably given similar instructions.

So the huge black horde spilled out over the green hills, the umHlanga, the umBonambi, the 6,000 young warriors of the inGobamakhosi, 'the humblers of kings', and all the others, every man eager for the first great conflict of Cetshwayo's reign. As spies brought news of their departure from Ulundi to the stolid redcoats tramping up from the Buffalo, an officer of the 24th scribbled in a quick letter home: 'Native reports from across the border say that Cetshwayo intends to eat up our columns one by one; I fear we have tough work before us.' A few days earlier the assembled officers of the same regiment had commemorated their forebears at Chillianwallah, where almost exactly thirty years before the 24th had lost over half its strength fighting the Sikhs. At the dinner table a toast had been drunk: 'That we may not get into such a mess, and have better luck this time.'

PART II

THE FIRST INVASION

4

Isandhlwana

No. 3 or Centre Column began crossing the Buffalo in thick mist and drizzling rain at 4.30 a.m. on 11 January. Covered by Lieutenant-Colonel Harness' battery of N/5 R.A., the advance was led by the mounted troops and the N.N.C., some of whom were drowned in the river, which came up to their necks. The less expendable battalions of the 24th were ferried across on flat-bottomed ponts, operated under the control of a subaltern of the Royal Engineers, Lieutenant Chard. A bridgehead was established without opposition and the whole day was spent getting the column across while Chelmsford rode north to confer with Colonel Evelyn Wood of the left column, the last opportunity he would have to do so. Reconnaissance showed that the track ahead would have to be reinforced where it crossed some marshland but, before the work could be undertaken by the Natal Pioneers, a Zulu kraal commanding the track had to be captured. This kraal belonged to Sihayo, whose execution of his errant wife had been one of the causes of Frere's ultimatum.

The task was given to the 1/3rd N.N.C., commanded by an Ulsterman, George Hamilton-Browne, a soldier of fortune who had served as a driver in the Royal Horse Artillery, in the Papal Zouaves, with colonial units in the Maori Wars of the 1860s, and in command of a hard-bitten gang of navvies turned irregular soldiers in the Kaffir War. He was thus thoroughly experienced in bush warfare, but had a near-total contempt for his new command, except for three of his companies formed from renegade Zulus. Encouraged by the bayonets of four supporting companies of the 1/24th, the 1/3rd N.N.C. attacked Sihayo's kraal on 12 January, and after a brief skirmish, in which only the Zulu companies showed to any advantage, the position was taken and a quantity of sheep and cattle captured.

The next few days were taken up with improving the track and getting the ponderous transport forward, while the mounted troops scouted forward in the direction of Isipezi Hill, led by an officer of the 12th Lancers, Lieutenant-Colonel Russell, who was seconded from his regiment. Russell reported that no Zulus were to be seen and that a suitable intermediate campsite with good fuel and water, from which a further advance could be made to the Isipezi, lay beneath a hill called Isandhlwana, some 10 miles along the track. Chelmsford decided to form an advanced base there so that some of the wagons could be off-loaded and sent back to Rorke's Drift for fresh supplies. At noon on 20 January, leaving the wagons to come on at their best speed, the column reached Isandhlwana and began setting up camp. As they marched in, many of the 24th must have noticed the similarity between the oddly-shaped hill and the badge of the Sphinx they wore on their collars.

Where No. 3 Column crossed the Buffalo. The post at Rorke's Drift is by the tree on the skyline to the left.

From its highest point just north of the track leading up from the Buffalo, the hill of Isandhlwana runs northwards for about 400 yards, until it drops sharply. The ground rises again for about 1,500 yards along a spur up to the Nqutu plateau. The plateau stretches north and eastwards towards the Isipezi Hill 10 miles away, thus forming the northern boundary to the plain which, some 4 miles wide, lies to the east of Isandhlwana and across which the track to Ulundi then ran. South of the track and forming the southern boundary of the plain lie the Malakata, Inhlazatye and Nkandhla hills, the former and westerly group running back to the Buffalo. Except where the spur runs down to Isandhlwana, the southern edge of the plateau forms an escarpment, broken at various places down which streams flow to join together on the plain, forming a number of wide ditches known as 'dongas' which cross the plain in a north-south direction. The narrowest begins about

600 yards due east of Isandhlwana. Some way south of the track it joins another, bigger donga, whose sources start on the plateau itself and whose main course flows about a mile from Isandhlwana. Between the narrow and big dongas the ground rises very slightly in a rocky crest. Beyond the big donga and a mile and a half due east of Isandhlwana is a prominent conical hill, with further on still another donga running down from a marked gap in the escarpment. Immediately south of Isandhlwana is a col, or 'nek', over which the track crossed and which rises on the other side to a stone-covered hill. West of the main hill back to the Buffalo the land is broken and seamed with water courses and ravines, but to the east it is wide open with no cover except among the boulders and the dongas. With its back to Isandhlwana, a force had a fine field of fire and observation reaching out to the escarpment, the conical hill and the Malakatas. Only where the

Natal Mounted Police with their baggage wagon during the advance of No. 3 Column. An engraving from the Illustrated London News.

northern spur joined the plateau was there an opportunity for an enemy to get round and strike in close to the hill.

The camp was formed under the eastern side of the hill in a north-south line with, at the farthest end from the track, the 2/3rd N.N.C., then, in order, 1/3rd N.N.C., 2/24th, N/5 R.A., the Mounted Volunteers, and the 1/24th just south of the track. The regimental transport was sited between each unit's camp and the hill, but the main wagon lines were on the nek behind the mounted camp, and the headquarters was behind the 2/24th. Infantry picquets were placed in an arc, half a mile out by day and a quarter by night, starting from the stony hill with the 1/24th, linking up with the 2/24th in the centre and the N.N.C. on the left up on the spur. By day mounted vedettes were sent far out to the edge of the plateau, the conical hill and south-east of the stony hill.

Conscious of Chelmsford's regulations for the force, Colonel Glyn, the column commander, proposed to enclose the camp within a laager, but Chelmsford himself forbade it, saying that it would take too long and that many of the wagons would be going back to Rorke's Drift. The standing orders for entrenching camps were not put into effect, probably because the stony ground would have made this very difficult, although breastworks could have been built with the rocks and boulders that scattered the area. Nor was any attempt made to construct an obstacle around the camp with thorn bushes and broken bottles. If an attack ensued, there was nothing to slow down the Zulu charge but infantry volleys and

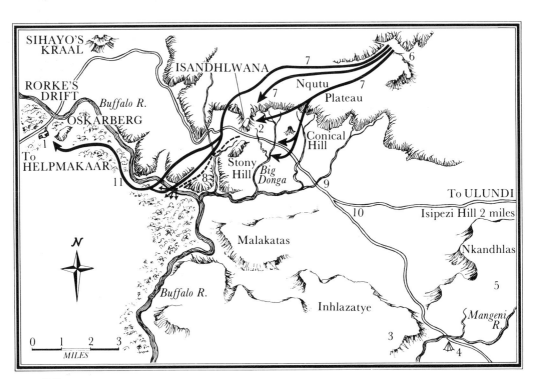

KEY

1. Rorke's Drift Mission Station
2. Camp at Isandhlwana
3. Dartnell's bivouac, 21–22 January
4. Site of new camp
5. Where Chelmsford breakfasted, 22 January
6. Ravine where Zulu impi found

7. Zulu attack on Isandhlwana
8. Fugitives' route to Buffalo
9. Where Hamilton-Browne watched attack on Isandhlwana
10. Where Chelmsford met Lonsdale
11. Zulu attack on Rorke's Drift

Operations at Isandhlwana and Rorke's Drift.

Officers of the 2nd Battalion, 24th Regiment before the war in 1878. Seated second from left in the second row is Henry Pulleine who commanded the 1st/24th at Isandhlwana.

gunfire. Several of the experienced 24th officers expressed concern about this. The adjutant of the 1/24th, Lieutenant Teignmouth Melvill, opined that: 'These Zulus will charge home, and with our small numbers we ought to be in laager, or, at any rate, be prepared to stand shoulder to shoulder.'

By the morning of the 22nd their numbers were even smaller, for Chelmsford had divided the force. The day before, conscious that Ulundi still lay 60 miles away and that he only had supplies for two months of which ten days had already passed, Chelmsford was more concerned with getting on and finding the Zulu Army than protecting a temporary camp. He had himself reconnoitred well to the east on the afternoon of the 20th without finding anything,

and on the 21st he sent out Major Dartnell with some eighty Natal Mounted Police and forty-seven of the Volunteers, supported by sixteen companies of the 3rd N.N.C. under Commandant Rupert Lonsdale, to scout the broken ground to the south-east. He sent another patrol to the Isipezi, while he himself had a look up on the Nqutu plateau; both patrols saw parties of Zulus but no sign of the main impi. In the late afternoon, when 10 miles from the camp, Dartnell encountered between 1,500 and 2,000 Zulus who after a skirmish withdrew to the north-east. As it was getting dark, Dartnell decided to bivouac for the night and sent back a messenger, asking for infantry reinforcements to be despatched so that he could attack in the morning.

When Chelmsford received this message at 1.30 in the morning, he formed the view that Zulus in the numbers and area reported by Dartnell must indicate that the main impi had reached the vicinity of Isipezi Hill sometime after the earlier patrol had left it. This put Dartnell, with only 100-odd mounted men and 1,600 N.N.C., in considerable danger, and Chelmsford decided to move out to his support. He ordered Glyn to assemble the 2/24th, less G Company which was on picquet, three-quarters of the Mounted Infantry (eighty-four men), four guns of N/5 and the company of Natal Pioneers to be ready to move as soon as it was light enough to march. To make up for the men he was taking from the camp, he sent a message to Durnford, whom he had earlier moved from Middle Drift to Rorke's Drift, to 'march to this camp at once with all the force you have with you of No. 2 Column'. The message also informed Durnford that Chelmsford was moving out with part of the column 'to attack a Zulu force about ten miles distant', but gave him no further orders.

The camp at Isandhlwana was to be left under the command of Brevet Lieutenant-Colonel Henry Pulleine, who had taken over the 1/24th when Glyn was appointed No. 3 Column Commander. Pulleine was aged forty but had seen no active service, having been employed on the staff during the Kaffir War. To defend the camp's 900-yard-long collection of tents, and well over a hundred wagons with all their draught animals, Pulleine had five companies of the 1/24th, F Company having joined the column the day before; G Company and the rear details of the 2/24th; 115 mounted men of the Police, Mounted Infantry and Volunteers; two guns of N/5 R.A.; Nos 6 and 9 Companies of 1/3rd N.N.C., Nos 4 and 5 Companies of 2/3rd N.N.C.; together with 13 staff officers and assorted administrative troops. In all he had 822 Europeans and 431 Africans, the backbone of the defence being the guns and the 597 rifles of the regular infantry.

Pulleine's orders were transmitted to him through Major Clery, Glyn's principal staff officer. In discussion of these orders, Clery impressed on Pulleine the need to keep his cavalry vedettes far out, to draw in his infantry outposts and to fight compact if he was attacked. He was to act strictly on the defensive and hold the camp. In addition he was to keep a wagon-load of ammunition at a scale of thirty rounds per man ready to send out to Glyn's force if required.

Chelmsford with Glyn's men reached Dartnell's bivouac at about 6.30 a.m. Their combined forces now totalled just over 2,500 men with four guns, of which 800 were Europeans, double the number left to hold Isandhlwana; the European element of both, however, was about equal. Dartnell had had an uneasy night but no impi had materialized. Chelmsford set the whole force searching the ground eastwards from Dartnell's bivouac towards the Mangeni River, but although the sweep flushed out a few parties of Zulus and some skirmishing occurred the enemy retreated further east, until by about 9.15 a.m. they had disappeared and nothing had been achieved. Chelmsford therefore called a halt for breakfast. He decided to establish Glyn's force in a new camp in the Mangeni valley and in due course bring forward Pulleine from Isandhlwana. Hamilton-Browne was ordered to return with his 1/3rd N.N.C. to Isandhlwana, searching the intervening ground as he went, and then escort the tentage and rations for Glyn's men back to the Mangeni. At 9.30 a galloper arrived with a message from Pulleine timed at 8.05 a.m.: 'Report just come in that the Zulus are advancing in force from left front of the camp.' Chelmsford read no urgency or cause for alarm in this message. He believed that Pulleine was strong enough to beat off any attack, and that even if he turned back now it would be 12.30 before the column could reach Isandhlwana, nearly five hours after the message had been despatched. He sent his naval A.D.C., Lieutenant Milne, to observe the camp through his telescope, but at 12 miles' range it

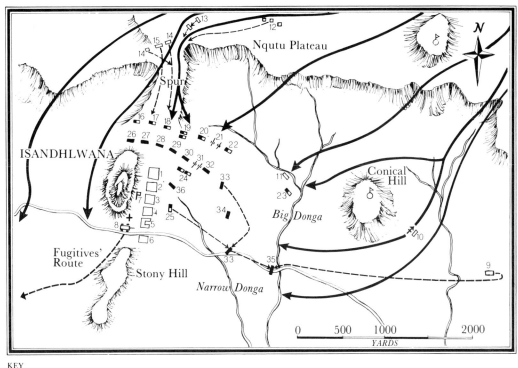

Battle of Isandhlwana

was difficult to make out any detail. Milne reported that he thought the oxen had been moved but that everything seemed normal. Chelmsford decided to stick to his plan for moving to the new campsite. Sending Hamilton-Browne on his way, preceded by Captain Gardner with a message for Pulleine to pack up the tents and rations for Glyn's troops, Chelmsford set off to reconnoitre the Mangeni valley, ordering Glyn to assemble his various units, now scattered over the hills, and to move in that direction. It was now about 10.30 a.m.

After Chelmsford had left at dawn, Pulleine had set out his protective screen. All the mounted men were deployed as vedettes on the high ground to the north-east and east. The infantry picquets were in an arc, with two companies of the 24th guarding the right front and flank, extended in posts of four men from the stony hill on the right round to the centre where their left met Captain J. Lonsdale's No. 9 Company, 1/3rd N.N.C., midway between the camp and the conical hill; the line was completed by Captain Barry's No. 5 Company,

51

The hill of Isandhlwana from the east. No. 3 Column's camp ran from left to right along the base of the hill.

2/3rd N.N.C., on the spur where it joined the plateau. A party under Lieutenant Anstey, 1/24th, was sent out to repair the track, and the rest of the camp settled down to its normal routine. Just before 8 a.m., as the men were having

road party and the 24th companies on picquet but leaving Lonsdale and Barry in position, and had the 'Fall in' sounded, forming all the 24th and the remaining N.N.C. companies, No. 6 of 1/3rd and No. 4 of 2/3rd, in column of companies in front of the camp. The mounted vedettes remained out on watch. Nothing further materialized for over an hour, however, when a few Zulus were seen briefly on the escarpment 3 miles away. A second message came down from the plateau to report that the force seen earlier had divided into three columns, two retiring to the north-east where they disappeared, and one moving to the north-west.

All remained quiet until 10.00 a.m. when Durnford rode up to Isandhlwana with five troops of Natal Native Horse. Some way behind him were Major Russell's Rocket Battery, two companies of the 1/1st N.N.C., Captain Nourse's (D) and Captain Stafford's (E), and his transport wagons. On the way up he had met Lieutenant Chard R.E., who had been at Isandhlwana when the second message had come in from the plateau and was returning to Rorke's Drift. On hearing Chard's news, particularly of the Zulu column thought to be moving north-west, Durnford had told him to hurry the Rocket Battery and Nourse's company on to Isandhlwana, leaving Stafford to escort the slow-moving wagons. Arriving at the camp, he sent Lieutenant Vause's troop of native horse back to reinforce Stafford. Russell and Nourse marched in about an hour later.

Durnford's arrival put Pulleine's position as camp commander in question. Not only was Durnford nine years older but, more importantly, he was three years senior; furthermore he had considerable experience of South Africa, having been in the country since 1872, and had gained a reputation for bravery in the Kaffir War where he had lost his left arm. Though his orders from Chelmsford had not been explicit about his relationship to Pulleine, or what he was to do on reaching Isandhlwana, the implication was that he was to act as a

breakfast, a trooper galloped down from the spur to report that a large force of Zulus was approaching from the north-east across the Nqutu plateau. Pulleine sent off the message Chelmsford was to receive at 9.30, called in the

A Troop of Mounted Infantry, c. 1879. Bandoliers replace the normal ammunition pouches.

reinforcement for the camp in the absence of Glyn's column, and by his seniority would automatically assume over-all command. Pulleine was willing to hand over responsibility but Durnford at once said that he and his command would not be staying in camp. He first sent the troops of Sikali Horse of Lieutenants Raw and Roberts, accompanied by Captain George Shepstone, his Political Assistant, and Captain Barton, up on to the plateau to clear it of scattered parties of Zulus. Barry's N.N.C. company was sent in support, being replaced on the spur by Captain Cavaye's E Company, 1/24th. The rest of the garrison was fallen out for their midday meal, while Durnford and Pulleine sat down for an early lunch.

At about the same time Hamilton-Browne, then driving his laggard battalion back to Isandhlwana but still some 9 miles from it, captured two Zulus, who told him the impi was close to the camp and was going to attack it. Browne at once sent a message back to Chelmsford, but its contents, and those of subsequent reports he sent over the next few hours, did not reach the General himself until about 2 p.m.

While Durnford and Pulleine were having lunch, a report reached them that some 500 Zulus to the north-east were moving away eastwards. Durnford decided to ride out with his two remaining troops, one of Basutos, the other of Christian Kaffirs from Edendale, plus the Rocket Battery and Nourse's company, to

Lieutenant-Colonel A. W. Durnford, Royal Engineers, commanding No. 2 Column.

and Nourse's Kaffirs. To the left, about a mile away and 200 feet above the camp, dots of red showed where Cavaye had extended his company at the head of the spur, with a section detached under Lieutenant Dyson 500 yards further west to watch the rear approaches to Isandhlwana. To Cavaye's right, above the escarpment, the files of Sikali Horse disappeared over the plateau, followed by Barry's N.N.C.

At about midday some of Raw's troop spotted some cattle being driven by Zulus up a slope about 4 miles north-east of the spur. They gave chase, only to see the Zulus disappear over the crest. On reaching the spot the leading trooper, finding himself suddenly on the edge of a deep ravine, pulled his horse up sharp. Looking into the ravine, he saw to his astonishment that which had eluded all the efforts of the past few days. Packed into the valley and all up its sides was a dense mass of Zulus sitting in complete silence. Here at last was the main impi, 20,000 of them, $5\frac{1}{2}$ miles north-east of the camp, and nearly 11 miles north of where Chelmsford had been searching fruitlessly all that morning.

The impi had not intended to attack until the following day and were resting in the ravine while small detachments sought food in the

head this force off so as to prevent them moving against Chelmsford (then proceeding towards the Mangeni), and asked Pulleine for the support of two companies of the 24th. Pulleine demurred, but under pressure yielded. His Adjutant, Melvill, however, protested so strongly at this further decrease to the camp's strength that Durnford agreed they should stay. Nevertheless, as he rode out of camp eastwards at about 11.30, his last words to Pulleine were that he would expect to be supported if he got into difficulties.

Except for sentries and men on duty, the troops in camp relaxed after their dinners, though still keeping their equipment on. To the front nothing moved under the noonday sun except for the distant vedettes and diminishing dust cloud of Durnford's horsemen, followed by Russell's slower-moving mule-borne battery

Major C. F. Clery, 32nd Regiment, Colonel Glyn's principal staff officer.

Tshingwayo (in white shirt), who commanded the impi at Isandhlwana, with his wives and attendants.

kraals that dotted the plateau. It was these that had been spotted by the vedettes during the morning. As the single rider wheeled his horse, however, the great black mass churned into life and started pouring up and over the rim. First out were the umCijo, umHlanga and some of the uThulwane, who set off in pursuit of Raw's troop, now alerted and falling back but firing as they went. On the Zulu right came the Nokenke and Nodwengu corps – umKhulutshane, uDududu and Isanqu – and to the left the young uVe, inGobamakhosi and the slightly older umBonambi. Further back in another ravine but also moving forward were the Undi corps and the uDhloko. A mile wide from wing to wing, this huge wave of warriors rolled south-west towards the escarpment at a steady run.

Roberts' troop added its fire to that of Raw's as they retired together, but the effect of 100 carbines fired from horseback was negligible against the oncoming horde. Barry's N.N.C. took to their heels. Captain Shepstone sent two Natal Carbineers of the vedette on the plateau galloping to the plain to warn Durnford, while he himself rode for the camp down the spur, shouting the news to Cavaye as he passed. Cavaye alerted Dyson on his left and opened fire when the Zulu right horn came into sight crossing his front.

Out on the plain Durnford was some 4 miles from the camp when he received a warning from Lieutenant Scott's vedette on the conical hill. At that moment he saw the Zulu left horn advancing over the skyline to his left front. They were still about 1,500 yards away but coming on fast. Durnford extended his two troops and opened fire when the Zulus were within range but, as on the plateau, the enemy advance was not even slowed down. He therefore began to retire slowly, one troop covering the other, while Russell's Rockets and Nourse's company, which had reached the conical hill, swung left and prepared to fire.

Back at the camp the firing on the plateau had already been heard when Shepstone galloped in at about 12.15. His arrival coincided with that of Captain Gardner, bearing Chelmsford's order for tents and rations for

Glyn's column. With the Zulus now appearing on the skyline, it was clearly no time to be loading wagons. Pulleine had the 'Alarm' sounded and scribbled a quick note for Chelmsford: 'Heavy firing to left of our camp. Cannot move camp at present.' To this Gardner added: 'Shepstone has come in for reinforcements, and reports the Basutos [sic] are falling back. The whole force at camp turned out and fighting about one mile to left flank.' This message was not to reach Chelmsford until about two and a half hours later. Having delivered his report, Shepstone rode back to join Raw and Roberts retiring from the plateau. Vause's troop and Stafford's N.N.C. company had recently arrived at the camp with Durnford's wagons and they went off with Shepstone. At the same time Pulleine sent Mostyn's F Company, 1/24th, up the spur to fill the gap between Dyson and Cavaye, who were now in extended order firing steadily at the Zulu right horn half a mile away.

There remained in camp Porteous' A, Younghusband's C, and Wardell's H Companies of the 1/24th, Pope's G Company of the 2/24th, to which were added the rear details of that battalion, two 7-pounders under Major Smith, R.A., Erskine's and Krohn's N.N.C. companies, and about thirty of the Newcastle Mounted Rifles under Captain Bradstreet. Lonsdale's N.N.C. company was still in position between the camp and the conical hill. As the garrison formed in front of the N.N.C. camp, the Zulus could be seen massing along the skyline about 2 miles to the north-east. Pulleine was in a dilemma. His recollection of Clery's orders to draw in a compact defence close to the hill conflicted with his undertaking to support Durnford, now fighting a rearguard action far out on the plain, and increasingly in danger of being cut off from the camp as the Zulus began spilling over the lip of the escarpment. If they reached the dead ground formed by the big donga west of the conical hill before Durnford passed it, he would surely be trapped, and furthermore it would

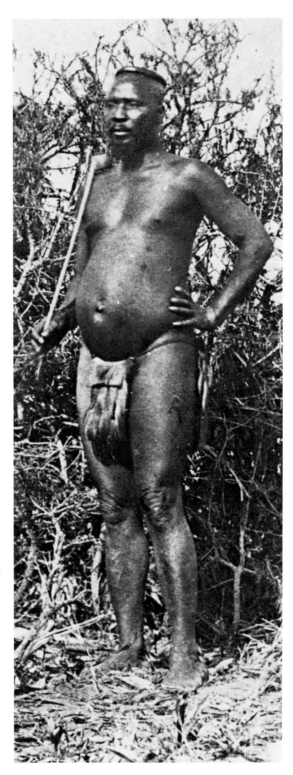

uSicwelewele, the commander of the inGoba-makhosi at Isandhlwana.

57

afford them cover to form up for a charge on the camp. Pulleine had already depleted his chances of a close defence by sending Mostyn and Cavaye up the spur, and he now compounded his error by his next deployment.

About 600 yards east of the N.N.C. camp, the rocky crest between the big and narrow dongas afforded some cover for riflemen and commanded the dead ground in the former. Here Smith's two guns were posted with the companies of Porteous and Wardell deployed on their left and right in skirmishing order, kneeling or lying behind the boulders. Some 400 yards to their right, Lonsdale's company was in a north-westerly tributary of the big donga. Further right still and reaching out towards the conical hill was Pope's company. On the left, Younghusband took up a position at the north end of Isandhlwana to cover the retirement of Mostyn and Cavaye, who fell back to form on his right front. As they did so, the Native Horse and N.N.C. from the plateau may have filled the gap between Cavaye and Porteous, at least for a time. The whole line, a mile and a half long from Younghusband on the left to Scott still on the conical hill to the east, faced north and north-east. The guns opened fire with shrapnel as the Zulus came boiling down the escarpment to the plain, joined by the riflemen when the range shortened to half a mile. The musketry of the left-hand companies caused heavy casualties among the Nokenke as they came running down the spur, and they retired back up the slope. In the centre the headlong advance of the umCijo and umHlanga was also checked when 400 yards from the line.

On the right, however, the enemy left horn overran Nourse's N.N.C. and Russell's Rocket Battery, continuing in pursuit of Durnford, who picked up Scott's vedette from the conical hill and rode hard for the big donga. On reaching it, he dismounted his men and lined the bank, opening fire on the uVe and inGobamakhosi as they swung westwards south of the conical hill. Bradstreet's mounted riflemen galloped down to join him. Their combined fire halted the

One of the 1/24th, 'no boy recruits but war-worn matured men, mostly with beards': No. 1313 Sergeant Thomas Cooper of H Company, killed at Isandhlwana.

inGobamakhosi in a mass below the conical hill, from where they were temporarily dispersed by the fire of one gun brought within range by Major Smith; this gun then returned to its former position. Seeing his right flank and rear threatened by the Zulu left horn, Pope

'The last order we heard given was, "Fix bayonets and die like British soldiers do", and so they did.' An impression of the final stand of the 24th at Isandhlwana as depicted for Victorian break-fast tables in the Graphic *of 15 March 1879.*

wheeled back G Company on to the rocky crest facing east, so that his left linked up with Wardell.

There is some doubt about the deployment of the N.N.C. companies at this time. A few survivors of Nourse's were in the donga with Durnford. It is highly unlikely that, in the face of the advance of the Zulu centre, Lonsdale's men would have held their exposed position between and slightly in front of Wardell and Pope's original line. Either they ran for it altogether or they fell back between Pope's new position and Durnford in the big donga. Many accounts have placed a body of N.N.C. in an angle between Cavaye and Porteous, just in front of the guns on Porteous' left. As mentioned above, some of the native troops from the plateau may have been in that area briefly, but one of the survivors of N/5, Lieutenant Curling, though he recalled having 24th companies on either side of his position, could remember no N.N.C. being near the guns.

Moreover, it would have been the natural inclination of the 24th officers to link up their companies so that the battalion could present as solid and united a front as possible to the enemy, and they would not have wished to have their line broken by elements of the N.N.C. in which few had any confidence. It would appear therefore that, directed either by Pulleine or by his second-in-command Degacher, or on their own initiative, Mostyn and Cavaye edged their companies sideways to the right, so that Cavaye's right was in touch with Porteous' left. This left a gap between Mostyn and Younghusband, who had his back to the north end of Isandhlwana itself, and this was filled, for a time at least, by Erskine's N.N.C. company and perhaps the Sikali Horse. Some of the companies of Barry and Stafford, which had been on the plateau, may have been here as well if they had not already made off. Krohn's remained in reserve near the tents. Thus, at about 1.30 p.m., Pulleine's line curved in an arc

Some of the officers of the 24th Regiment who fell at Isandhlwana. From left to right, top: Lt-Col. H. B. Pulleine, Captain W. E. Mostyn; centre: Lieutenants H. J. Dyer, T. L. G. Griffith, E. H. Dyson; bottom: Captain C. W. Cavaye, Lieutenant E. O. Anstey.

60

from the north end of Isandhlwana to a point on the rocky crest 600 yards due east of the centre of the camp, with Durnford's men forward to the right holding the donga.

In the face of the 24th's steady musketry the Zulu advance wavered, the warriors lying down about 400 yards in front of the line. Nearly fifty years later General Smith-Dorrien, who in 1879 was a subaltern on the staff of the column, remembered the 24th as 'no boy recruits but war-worn matured men, mostly with beards. Possessed of splendid discipline and sure of success, they lay on their position making every round tell.' Each time the Zulus rose from cover, the fire drove them to earth again. Those Zulus armed with rifles kept up a heavy fusillade, hitting a few men in the line, but most of their rounds passed overhead, falling in the camp area. Quartermaster Bloomfield of the 2/24th was killed by one of these shots while loading ammunition on to a mule-cart. So far, however, casualties had been slight.

Though the 24th were holding the Zulu advance, Durnford far out on the right was running short of ammunition. He sent back his two troop leaders, Davies and Henderson, for more, but these, not knowing the location of their own reserve wagons, which had reached the camp after they had ridden out, went to the nearest, that of the 1/24th, whose quartermaster refused them, his responsibility being to his own battalion. In their absence the whole impi rose for a general advance. The centre was again halted some 150 yards short of the line by the 24th companies closing up and firing volleys. The left horn, however, wavering away from Durnford's last few rounds and cross-fire from Pope's company, extended to its left to encircle Durnford's right. When Davies and Henderson returned empty-handed, Durnford, now out of ammunition and seeing the Zulus outflanking him, ordered his men to mount up and, abandoning the donga, rode for the camp to form a new line on the right front of the tents while the officers again went in search of more supplies of ammunition.

Many accounts of this stage of the battle have attributed what happened next to ammunition failing to reach the firing line, with much emphasis on incompetent and selfish quartermasters and their inability to open the reserve ammunition boxes. There is little doubt that Durnford's men ran out of ammunition and had difficulty in obtaining more. It was not unnatural that the quartermaster of the 1/24th, whose entire service life had been spent in the close confines of his regiment, was reluctant to hand over his reserves when he could see the hard fight his own men were having. His own re-supply problem was made more difficult by the distance between his wagons and the 24th companies. On the other hand, it seems unlikely that a good battalion like the 1/24th, experienced in the Kaffir War and with the regulations about re-supply laid down by Chelmsford fixed in their minds, would not have made adequate arrangements beforehand. Whatever the truth of the matter, Durnford's withdrawal had suddenly imperilled the entire line, which up to this point had been holding the Zulus at bay and inflicting punishing losses upon them.

Just before the Native Horse retired, Pope, seeing that Durnford was in difficulties, advanced his company south-east to reinforce the donga. Before he could reach it, Durnford rode off. Pope had to fall back, taking up a new position just north of the track between the big and narrow dongas, and re-opening fire on the left horn, part of which was sweeping round south of the track and advancing under cover of a herd of oxen towards the 1/24th's tents. Pope's move, however well intentioned, had exposed the right of the main line. There may have been some N.N.C. of Lonsdale's and other companies in the gap on Wardell's right, but if they were still there the sight of the Zulus in the donga and pressing forward on the right ensured that they did not remain. Now, with only Pope's ninety-odd men between the camp and the Zulu left horn, and a gap of about 700 yards between him and Wardell, the entire

1/24th were in danger of being outflanked. Pulleine ordered the 'Retire' to be sounded.

As the 24th companies fell back on the camp, probably in rallying squares and firing as they went, the Zulus everywhere rushed forward. Being only 100–300 yards from the line when the bugle blew, they reached the guns, which had been firing case-shot, before N/5 could limber up. After a fierce flurry of hand-to-hand fighting, Smith managed to get the guns away. As for the infantry, a Zulu, Uguku, later recalled that, as he and his comrades rushed forward, 'the soldiers retired on the camp, fighting all the way, and as they got into the camp, we were intermingled with them'.

For some time there had been a steady trickle of camp-followers and the odd N.N.C. heading back over the nek towards the Buffalo and safety. Now it became a flood. Krohn's company, the last reserve, and the remaining N.N.C. fled rearwards. The Native Horse, which had fought well, but without ammunition could do no more, galloped away, as did those of the Mounted Infantry and Volunteers who still had a horse. On the far side of the nek, however, they found their way barred by the Zulu right horn, which had come round the west side of Isandhlwana, and consequently had to bear off south-westwards down a ravine which led ultimately to the Buffalo, some 4 miles away. They were harried on the right by the Nodwengu corps and on the left by the inGobamakhosi, who had come round the stony hill, but eighty-five Europeans, of which just under half were regulars, chiefly of N/5 and the Mounted Infantry, eventually reached safety at Helpmakaar. Most of the Basuto and Edendale troops got clear, and by opening fire on the pursuing Zulus at the river bank enabled others to do so. Many of the N.N.C. hurriedly divested themselves of anything connecting them with the column and made their escape. The gun detachments of N/5 fought their way through the camp, losing fifty men in an attempt to save the guns, but further on one gun overturned and the other was halted by a ravine.

As the horsemen and native infantry made their bid for life, back under Isandhlwana the 24th fought to the end. When the field was searched later, only the bodies of one colour-sergeant and twenty men of the regiment were found on the rocky crest. Casualties began to fall at the line of tents as the men retreated through the camp, fighting hand-to-hand, but in and around the 1/24th camp at the end of the line several groups stood their ground and fought till they were killed. Durnford and possibly Pulleine fell close to the track on the nek where some thirty of the 24th and a similar number of Police and Natal Carbineers made a stand. Others fought it out among the dongas on the western slopes. When their ammunition ran out they defended themselves with their bayonets. Uguku said: 'We were quite unable to break their square until we had killed a great many of them by throwing our assegais at short distances. We eventually overcame them this way.'

Probably the last group to die were Younghusband's C Company of which some sixty men, including two other officers, held out for a long time on the lower slopes of Isandhlwana. The Zulus said that finally 'the soldiers gave a shout and charged down upon us. There was an inDuna in front with a long flashing sword, which he whirled round his head as he ran. They killed themselves running down, for our people got above them and quite surrounded them.' One man was believed to have held out until evening, firing from a cave high among the rocks.

Of the entire six companies of the 24th only two bandsmen and Colonel Glyn's groom escaped, to which must be added three serving with the Rocket Battery and four with the Mounted Infantry. The 2/24th had brought their Colours into the field; these had been left in the camp when Glyn's force marched out in the morning and were never seen again. The 1/24th had only the Queen's Colour, the Regimental having been left in Natal. Some time before the end, the Adjutant, Melvill, being mounted, was

'The Last of the 24th – Isandhlwana.' A painting by R. T. Moynan.

Lieutenants T. Melvill (above) and N. J. A. Coghill (right), 24th Regiment, awarded the Victoria Cross posthumously for attempting to save the Queen's Colour of the 1/24th after Isandhlwana.

Top: The drift across the Buffalo where most of the fugitives from Isandhlwana crossed into Natal.

Private Samuel Wassall, 80th Regiment attached to the Mounted Infantry, who won the Victoria Cross for saving a comrade under fire at the Buffalo River after Isandhlwana.

ordered to carry it to safety. He rode off down the fugitives' ravine where he was joined by another officer of the regiment, Lieutenant Coghill, who, having injured his knee two days beforehand and being unable to walk, had been acting as a mounted staff officer. On reaching the river Coghill got across, but Melvill was unhorsed in mid-stream. Seeing him struggling to swim with the Colour, Coghill rode back into the water to help him. Zulus were firing from the bank and Coghill's horse was killed. They managed to reach the Natal bank but being exhausted they stopped to rest. Here they were caught and killed. The Colour for which both had died fell into the Buffalo but was recovered some months later. Weeks afterwards their combined attempt to save the Colour was honoured by posthumous awards of the Victoria Cross. Apart from Private Wassall of the 80th, serving with the Mounted Infantry, who won the same decoration for saving a drowning comrade while crossing the Buffalo under fire, these were the only Crosses awarded for Isandhlwana. Many other brave acts had no living witnesses.

The last hours at Isandhlwana had been seen from afar by Hamilton-Browne, whose battalion was about 5 miles from camp when the main impi was discovered on the plateau. He heard the guns open fire at 12.30, as Chelmsford had also heard them, and sent a message back with a European sergeant. He pressed on until about half an hour later he saw large numbers of Zulus between him and the camp; these must have been the left horn advancing across the plain to the east of the conical hill. He despatched his third message to Chelmsford and swung left to try to approach the camp from the south. At 1.30 he saw Smith's gun moved from the rocky crest to open fire on the Zulu left horn, then temporarily halted by Durnford south of the conical hill. Shortly after, when he saw the left horn advancing behind the oxen towards the nek, he sent off Captain Develin with his last message: 'For God's sake come back, the camp is surrounded and things, I fear, are going badly.' At about 2 p.m. he could see that the fighting was now within the camp itself, but as he then became aware of more Zulus crossing his front he deemed it prudent, in view of the uncertain calibre of his battalion of which only about a tenth had rifles with a mere fifteen rounds, to retire on some rocky ground to his left rear. As far as he could tell, it was all over in the camp by 2.30 p.m.

At least two of Hamilton-Browne's first three messengers encountered the Mounted Infantry patrolling under Lieutenant-Colonel Russell, who sent out parties to find Chelmsford,

but without success. Develin came up with Lieutenant-Colonel Harness who was halted with his two sections of N/5 R.A. and an escort of the 2/24th, waiting for orders. Harness turned his command about and set off for Isandhlwana, sending one of his officers back to find the elusive Chelmsford. The latter eventually received Develin's alarming message probably at about 2.30 p.m. Although he was aware that action of some sort had been occurring at the camp, he had hitherto received no reports other than that sent by Pulleine at 8 a.m. He was therefore unconvinced by Hamilton-Browne's report, so much so that he countermanded Harness' return to Isandhlwana. Some ten minutes later he met Russell, who told him of the earlier messages. Chelmsford decided he would ride back and see for himself, taking the Mounted Infantry as escort but leaving the rest of Glyn's column concentrated at the campsite. He had not long started when another rider appeared with the report sent by Pulleine and Gardner at 12.15 p.m. When he reached Hamilton-Browne, for whom he had little regard, the latter stated that the camp was lost, but Chelmsford still refused to believe it. Not until about 3.30 did he finally grasp the full extent of the disaster. The commander of the 3rd N.N.C., Commandant Rupert Lonsdale, a different figure from the company commander of the same name who had perished at Isandhlwana, had gone out with Dartnell on the 21st. Feeling unwell, he had started riding slowly back to Isandhlwana on his own during the morning of the 22nd. In his feverish condition and part-stupefied by the sun, he had almost ridden into the camp before he realized that it was full of victorious Zulus. Horrified, he galloped back the way he had come, finally meeting Chelmsford when the latter was still some 4½ miles from Isandhlwana and convincing him that Pulleine's force had been destroyed.

Chelmsford immediately decided to re-take the camp. He sent a staff officer back to summon up Glyn and despatched the Mounted

Manning the defences at Helpmakaar where the fugitives from Isandhlwana sought safety. An Illustrated London News *engraving after a sketch by Lieutenant W. W. Lloyd, 24th Regiment.*

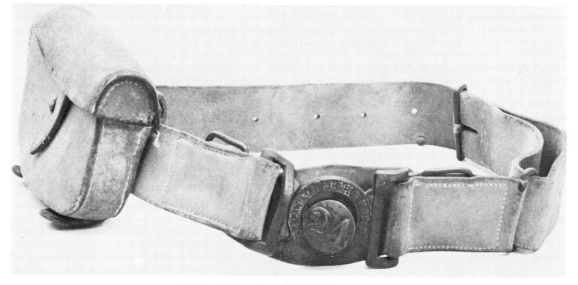

Waistbelt and pouch, 24th Regiment.

The Battle of Isandhlwana. Painting by Charles E. Fripp. The Regimental Colour shown in the painting could not have been there as that of the 1/24th had been left at Helpmakaar and both Colours of the 2/24th were in a tent.

Infantry forward to reconnoitre. The latter reported an hour later that the Zulus had been looting and burning the camp but that many were making off up the Nqutu plateau. Marching at best speed Glyn's column reached Chelmsford at just after 6 p.m. Having made a short speech to his troops, Chelmsford ordered the advance with the 2/24th around the guns in the centre and the Volunteers and Mounted Infantry on either wing. By the time they approached Isandhlwana it was dark, so the young soldiers of the 2/24th were mercifully spared the sight of the ghastly remains of their sister battalion. Not a sound could be heard, and after the guns had fired at the nek and three companies had been sent up the stony hill without drawing any reaction, it was clear that the Zulus had gone. Nothing more could be done in the darkness so Chelmsford ordered the force to bivouac for the night in a position of all-round defence. For the General, and indeed for the entire column, the blow must have been shattering. Over 1,200 men had been left in camp, reinforced by nearly 500 of Durnford's, and now not a soul remained alive. Then, as they tried to get a fitful rest, someone heard a distant musketry towards the west, and a dull red glow could be seen above Rorke's Drift.

5
Rorke's Drift

After No. 3 Column had marched off with high hopes into Zululand, leaving a disgruntled B Company of the 2/24th to guard the crossing at Rorke's Drift, its commander, Lieutenant Gonville Bromhead, found that he was also responsible for the safety of the column's hospital and commissariat store. The former had been established in the Oskarberg Mission House belonging to the Reverend Otto Witt, where thirty-three sick and injured men of various units were cared for by Surgeon-Major Reynolds with three men of the Army Hospital Corps and a chaplain, the Reverend George Smith.

On the 12th three wounded men, including a Swiss N.C.O. of the N.N.C., Corporal Schiess, were brought in after the skirmish at Sihayo's kraal. Acting-Commissary Dalton, a fifty-year-old ex-sergeant-major of the 85th, and Acting-Storekeeper Byrne presided over the stores in the only other building, formerly Witt's small, stone-built chapel. At the Drift itself, a quarter of a mile away to the north, Lieutenant Chard, R.E., supervised the ponts with Sergeant Milne of the 2/3rd Buffs and one sapper. With the 84 men of B Company and 6 of the 1/24th who had been left behind on various duties, there were thus 137 men, including the hospital patients. There was also an unruly and undisciplined company of Natal Kaffirs under a colonial officer, Captain Stephenson, and some European

N.C.O.s who seemed little better than their men. They brought the total numbers at the post up to just above 200.

Lieutenant J. R. M. Chard, V.C., Royal Engineers, who assumed command of the post at Rorke's Drift.

The mission station at Rorke's Drift. A photograph taken after the fight from the Oskarberg terraces looking north-west. The remains of the burnt-out hospital have been removed and only the storehouse, with unthatched roof, and the cattle kraal remain.

RORKE'S DRIFT, NATAL. Night of 22ᴺᴰ January, 1879

A contemporary sketch of the defences of Rorke's Drift, looking south-east with the Oskarberg behind. A = Commissariat Store. B = The Hospital. C = The perimeter wall of mealie bags between the hospital and the cattle kraal. The rear wall of mealie bags and the two wagons can be seen behind. D = The transverse wall of biscuit boxes. E = The mealie bag redoubt.

Men of B Company, 2/24th Regiment which held Rorke's Drift. The blurred figure at left is Lieutenant G. Bromhead, V.C. A photograph taken at the end of the war.

Dabulamanzi, who commanded the Zulus at Rorke's Drift.

Some of the men who won the Victoria Cross at Rorke's Drift:

*Surgeon-Major J. H. Reynolds,
Army Medical Department.*

*Corporal W. Allen, 24th,
taken after his promotion to sergeant.*

Private F. Hitch, 24th.

Private H. Hook, 24th.

Private W. Jones, 24th.

Private J. Williams, 24th.

Private R. Jones, 24th.

*Assistant-Commissary J. L. Dalton,
Commissariat and Transport Department.*

The hospital, with stone and brick walls, a thatched roof and a verandah stood on a low rocky ledge facing north-west. Inside it was divided by mud-brick walls into eleven small rooms, some little bigger than cupboards, four of which on the side and rear only had doors to the outside. At a distance of 35 yards and slightly to the rear stood the storehouse with, to its right front and almost adjoining, a stone cattle kraal with walls 4 feet high. To the east, 200 yards away, were the slopes of the Oskarberg terraces, 500 feet high, which completely dominated the rear of the post.

Early on the morning of the 22nd, after an uneventful ten days, Chard, who though senior in the Army to Bromhead was only responsible for the crossing place and ponts, rode up to Isandhlwana. While there he heard the report that one body of the Zulus seen earlier on the plateau was moving away north-

west, so he decided to return to Rorke's Drift, passing Durnford's column on his way back. After lunching with Bromhead he was back with his ponts, when at about 2.30 two European officers of the N.N.C., Adendorff and Vane, galloped across the Buffalo. They told Chard that the camp at Isandhlwana had been wiped out and that about 4,000 Zulus were advancing to attack Rorke's Drift.

Since the post was entirely undefended, Chard and Bromhead briefly considered whether they should not retire on Helpmakaar where there were two companies of the 1/24th. They decided that, in view of the impossibility of defending two slow-moving ox wagons crammed with sick and wounded while on the march, there was nothing for it but to stand and fight. Aided by Dalton, they hurriedly devised and built an all-round rampart about 4 feet high linking the hospital and storehouse, using

A sketch made on the spot by Lt-Col. J. N. Crealock of Lt-Col. Russell's Mounted Infantry riding up to Rorke's Drift on the morning of 23 January. Men of the garrison are waving from the storehouse roof.

74

mealie bags from the store and incorporating the two wagons. The hospital walls were loopholed and six men told off for its garrison. Rifles were issued to those of the sick who were capable of using them, ammunition was made ready, and Private Hitch of B Company was posted as a look-out astride the storehouse roof. By about 4.30 p.m. a roughly rectangular perimeter about 150 yards long and 20–30 yards wide had been constructed. Bromhead allotted firing positions around the perimeter to his company and any others capable of bearing arms, including Stephenson's Kaffirs who had rifles; those with only assegais were placed in the stone kraal.

About an hour earlier Lieutenant Vause and his troop of Native Horse had ridden up, having escaped more or less unscathed from Isandhlwana. Chard had asked Vause to place some of his men to watch the crossing; others guarded the flanks of the Oskarberg which obscured the view south-east towards Fugitive's Drift 2 miles downstream, from which area Vane had reported that the advancing Zulus were likely to come. At about 5 p.m. George Smith, who had been observing with a telescope from the top of the Oskarberg, spotted the enemy crossing the river and shouted a warning. Almost simultaneously Vause's troop galloped past the post without stopping, heading for Helpmakaar, and causing a panic among Stephenson's Kaffirs, who decamped in a body with their commander. At a stroke the strength of the garrison had been reduced by more than half, and there were now only about 100 men fit enough to defend the 400-yard perimeter. Chard at once withdrew men from the line to construct an inner barricade of biscuit boxes between the western end of the storehouse and the north wall. Work had just started on the second layer of boxes when Hitch shouted from the roof and the first mass of Zulus swarmed round the western end of the Oskarberg.

All were mature warriors of three regiments from Dabulamanzi's Undi corps which, apart from harrying the fugitives, had not been engaged at Isandhlwana: the bachelor inDlu-yengwe, aged about thirty and 1,000 strong, the 2,500 uDloko, aged forty and about 1,000 of the uThulwane, aged forty-five, the two latter both of married men. While some Zulu riflemen climbed up on the Oskarberg to fire down into the post, the inDlu-yengwe in the lead hurled themselves at the south wall. Though they came on with great courage, the volleys from the Martini-Henrys at close range inflicted heavy casualties. After a while, finding no cover in which to shelter from the fire, the inDlu-yengwe surged back to join the other two regiments who were now attacking the west end of the hospital and the left front of the north wall, spilling further along the wall as they were repulsed, to try to clamber in over the mealie bags. Charge succeeded charge but everywhere the defenders stood firm, firing as fast as they could reload and thrusting with their long bayonets against the stabbing assegais.

Inside the perimeter Chard and Bromhead, assisted by Commissary Dalton, all armed themselves with rifles and bayonets and moved constantly up and down the line, encouraging the men and adding their own fire at any point where casualties caused a gap. Ammunition was being expended at a rapid rate, but Chaplain Smith, aided by wounded men who could no longer man the walls, kept the firers replenished from the boxes placed in front of the storehouse. Numbers of men along the north wall were hit in the back by fire from the Oskarberg, but every man was attended to by Surgeon-Major Reynolds who worked ceaselessly in a makeshift surgery set up in the storehouse.

By 6 p.m., after half an hour's fierce fighting, the immense pressure on the left front of the perimeter forced the defenders between the hospital verandah and the north wall to fall back behind a short dog-leg wall linking the east end of the hospital with the main rampart. This left the hospital forming a vulnerable salient. Though its six defenders and a few of the sick had been firing furiously from their loopholes, their field of fire was limited, and with the main pressure building up at this end of the post Chard decided to evacuate the hospital.

While the men lining the dog-leg and north and south walls fought on against the persistent Zulu rushes, the hospital defenders began to tunnel a route to the east end through the inner partitions of the unconnected rooms at the back. As the western end was abandoned, the Zulus broke in so that the evacuation became a fighting withdrawal in miniature, two or three men holding off the furious warriors while others behind them dug with their bayonets and helped the patients through the gaps into the yard beyond. For over two hours Privates Cole, Hook, Joseph and John Williams, and Robert and William Jones kept up their devoted work. From 6.45 they faced an additional danger when the Zulus set the thatched roof alight, but they battled on amid the flames. At the far end, Corporal Allen and Private Hitch, though both wounded, helped the patients through the final opening and covered their often painful progress across the yard to the storehouse.

Soon after 7 p.m. their passage became even more perilous when Chard decided he would have to abandon the left half of the north wall and fall back behind the transverse barricade of biscuit boxes. The Zulus were packed in front of the hospital and the struggle along the north wall was hand-to-hand. The defenders had been fighting at close quarters for an hour and a half without a let-up and were beginning to tire. The mealie bag rampart was collapsing under the press of Zulu bodies hurled against it. By falling back Chard reduced his perimeter to a circumference of 170 yards, of which the back wall of the storehouse formed an impenetrable barrier. The evacuation of the hospital, however, could now only be covered by fire from the transverse wall.

Despite heavy losses the Zulu charges never faltered and they came on again and again at the north wall. As long as the mealie bags held firm, their height above the ledge gave the defenders an advantage over the Zulus who could only stab upwards as the soldiers leaned over to fire or thrust with their bayonets. Nevertheless Chard realized that, with the overwhelming numbers against him and with his own force diminished by casualties, the new perimeter could not hold for ever. He therefore withdrew some men from the fighting line to start building an 8-foot high redoubt backing on to the stone kraal, using the last piles of mealie bags lying in front of the storehouse.

Darkness had fallen but the whole ferocious scene was lit by the blazing hospital. Eventually the roof fell in just as the last patients were got out and the heroic defenders dashed across the yard. Cole, Joseph Williams and seven of the patients had been killed and others wounded, but twenty-two were saved. The sick and badly wounded men were placed in the bottom of the redoubt, which was lined by twenty marksmen.

While the fight still raged along the transverse and north walls, the Zulus next tried to break in over the stone kraal. It was darker here and another broken-down kraal outside the perimeter afforded them some cover. By 10.30 the kraal had to be abandoned and the surviving defenders were all packed between the transverse wall and the western wall of the kraal. They were tired out, their rifles were too hot to hold, the brass cartridges were jamming and everyone was parched with thirst. At about 11.45 Chard led a bayonet charge over the transverse wall to haul in a water cart which stood in the yard. Still the Zulus came on far into the night, each onslaught being met with bullet and bayonet. At last, some time after 2 a.m., their efforts became more half-hearted and finally died down. By 4 a.m. the hospital had burned itself out, the Zulus had pulled back, and silence descended on the tiny perimeter, as the smoke-blackened, exhausted handful of defenders ceased fire and rested for the first time in ten hours' fighting.

At dawn, an hour and a half later, the growing light revealed the piles of Zulu dead in and around the battered and almost demolished

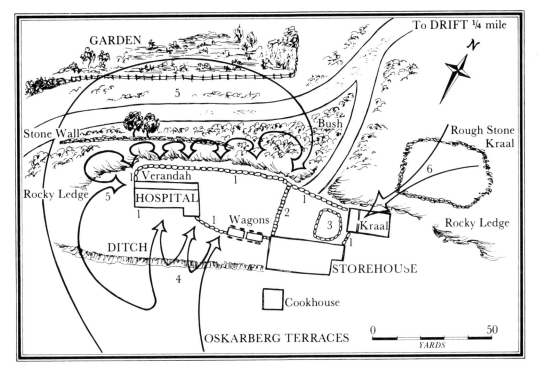

GARDEN

To DRIFT ¼ mile

N

5

Stone Wall

Bush

Rough Stone
Kraal

6

Rocky Ledge   5

Verandah   1

HOSPITAL

1

1

1   Wagons

2

1

3   Kraal

Rocky Ledge

1

DITCH

4

STOREHOUSE

Cookhouse

OSKARBERG TERRACES

0   50

YARDS

KEY

1. Initial Perimeter formed by mealie bag ramparts, 2 wagons and
   walls of hospital, storehouse and kraal
2. Transverse wall of biscuit boxes
3. Mealie bag redoubt

4. First Zulu attack
5. Main Zulu attack
6. Last Zulu attack

The Defence of Rorke's Drift.

ramparts of the post. The number of corpses counted in the immediate vicinity was 370, and in the days that followed scores more would be discovered in the neighbourhood. Fifteen of the garrison had been killed, two were dying, seven others were badly wounded and most of the rest had minor injuries; all were at the end of their strength. Twenty thousand rounds had been fired, and if the Zulus came on again there would be little hope of holding them. At 7 a.m. the impi suddenly reappeared to the west of the Oskarberg. With sinking hearts the garrison again manned the defences, but after a while the Zulus made off, keeping well out of range. They too were exhausted, many were wounded and all were hungry. Dabulamanzi's incursion into Natal against Cetshwayo's orders had achieved nothing and now they were heading for home. An hour later the alarm was again raised when movement was spotted across the Buffalo, but not long afterwards Russell's Mounted Infantry came galloping up to the post, followed by Chelmsford and Glyn's column. Chelmsford had moved his men off from Isandhlwana before first light to spare them the sights of the disaster. As they had marched back towards the Buffalo, the sight of Zulus some way off and moving in the opposite direction had increased his forebodings as to the fate of Rorke's Drift. It was therefore with great relief that he found that the post had held out. Unaware that Cetshwayo had forbidden any invasion of Natal, it seemed that Chard, Bromhead and their men had saved the colony.

Their magnificent stand also went some way to redeeming the fiasco of Isandhlwana, and the reputations of Chelmsford, Bartle Frere, the Army and indeed the British Government in the

Group of Natal Native Contingent at Rorke's Drift after the battle. The storehouse is on the sky-line to the right, the Oskarberg terraces to the left.

eyes of the electorate. It is not surprising, therefore, that the defence of Rorke's Drift was subsequently rewarded by an unprecedented number of Victoria Crosses for a single action. Nevertheless, even if such generosity was motivated by political expediency, it in no way detracts from the valour and stubborn endurance of B Company, 2/24th Regiment and the other men who held the post, nor from the deeds of those who actually received the Cross: Lieutenants Chard and Bromhead, Corporal Allen, Privates Hitch, Hook, R. Jones, W. Jones and John Williams, Surgeon-Major Reynolds, Assistant-Commissary Dalton and Corporal Schiess, the Swiss N.C.O. of the N.N.C., who, though wounded before the action began and again during it, never left his post. The Reverend George Smith was made a permanent Chaplain to the Forces.

At Isandhlwana the combined forces of Pulleine and Durnford had been outnumbered ten to one by the Zulu regiments actually engaged. Fighting in the open, and despite being supported by artillery, they had been overwhelmed in some two hours. The defenders of Rorke's Drift, though facing odds of nearly forty to one, had held out successfully for about ten hours. Their achievement said much for their hastily improvised ramparts.

Chelmsford's carefully prepared invasion plan lay in ruins. With the destruction of No. 3 Column there was nothing for it but to fall back into Natal and start again. Furthermore, with the threat to Ulundi through the centre of Zululand now removed, the Zulu Army could concentrate against either of the flanking columns, and any progress these had been able to make was rendered null and void.

6

Eshowe and Gingindhlovu

No. 1 Column at the Lower Drift had been ordered to establish an advanced base at Eshowe, 37 miles away, prior to continuing its advance on Ulundi. Colonel Pearson, the column commander, had at his disposal just under 5,000 men, of which 2,250 were Natal Kaffirs of Major Graves' 2nd N.N.C. and the Native Pioneer Corps. His mounted force totalled 312 of the Mounted Infantry and Natal Volunteers, all under the command of Major Barrow, 19th Hussars. The supply train consisted of 384 ox wagons and nearly 3,400 baggage animals with some 600 civilian wagoners and drivers.

The column began crossing the Tugela by pont on 12 January, covered by the Naval Brigade of 200 sailors and marines until Barrow's men were over and could take up the task of protection. The next five days were occupied in ferrying the wagons across, while a second fort, Tenedos, was constructed on the Zulu bank to complement Fort Pearson, which had already been built on the Natal side. As mentioned earlier, garrisons of the Naval Brigade, two companies of the 99th and a company of N.N.C. were told off to occupy both forts.

The way ahead ran at first over gently sloping grasslands but then began to rise up steep, scrub-covered hills, seamed with dongas and traversed by the three small rivers that would have to be negotiated before Eshowe was reached. It had been raining steadily for several days, turning the track surface into mud, and since the steep banks of the dongas would slow up the progress of the transport Pearson decided to advance in two divisions, each a day's march apart. A few Zulus in scattered groups had been encountered by Barrow's patrols but none in any numbers.

Early on the 18th Pearson set off with the first division: five companies of his own battalion, the 2/3rd Buffs, the rest of the Naval Brigade with their guns, rockets and a Gatling, the 7-pounders of 11/7 Battery under Lieutenant Lloyd, Captain Wynne's field company Royal Engineers, about 150 of the mounted men and the 1/2nd N.N.C.; 2,400 men in all with 50 wagons. They would be followed on the next day by the second division under Lieutenant-Colonel Welman of the 99th, with four companies of that regiment, the remaining three of the Buffs, the 2/2nd N.N.C., and the balance of the cavalry: 2,000 men with 80 wagons. The rest of the transport was to be moved forward later.

The advance proceeded smoothly if slowly, owing to difficulties in getting the wagons across the swollen drifts, and by the evening of the 21st the force was camped 4 miles south of the Inyezane River, having that afternoon burned a deserted military kraal at Gingindhlovu. The march was resumed early next morning and, after crossing the Inyezane

*H.M.S.*Tenedos *detachment of the Naval Brigade with No. 1 Column. Note the Royal Marines in glengarries to the right of the group.*

without much trouble, Pearson halted his division for breakfast in an area of scrub, beyond which the track began its climb up the hills towards the plateau on which Eshowe was situated.

Immediately ahead was a steep ridge from which three spurs ran down to the Inyezane. The track wound up the central spur and over the crest, passing a prominent knoll about halfway up and a small kraal on the left near the crest.

Just after 8 a.m., as the men were finishing their breakfasts, a few Zulus appeared near the knoll. A company of N.N.C. under Lieutenant Hart was sent up the spur after them. Before he could reach them, they disappeared into the thick scrub of the ravine to the right, only to reappear later on the right-hand spur. Hart set off in pursuit, but on gaining the far spur he had to halt to reform his company, which had become disordered passing across the ravine. As he was doing so, a mass of Zulus suddenly appeared over the crest and began pouring down the spur.

It will be remembered that, when the main impi had left Ulundi on the 17th, a smaller one, 6,000 strong, had been sent south. It was this force, the umXapo, Iqwa, Nsugamgeni,

Ngwekwe and Ngulubi, that now barred Pearson's advance. It had been lying in wait behind the crest but the advance of Hart's company had precipitated the left horn into a premature attack. At the sight of it swarming down the slope, Hart's Kaffirs fled into the ravine, leaving their European officers and N.C.O.s to make a fruitless stand before they were swept aside as the Zulus headed for the scrub at the foot of the spur, beyond which the wagons were assembling as they crossed the drift.

As soon as Hart opened fire, the Naval Brigade with the Gatling and two companies of the Buffs, supported by Lloyd's 7-pounders, were pushed up on the central spur to the area of the knoll, where they opened fire across the ravine at the long column of Zulus. Around the wagons Barrow hastily formed a firing line with his mounted men, Wynne's sappers and two more Buffs' companies which had been escorting the transport, ready to engage the Zulus as they charged out of the scrub. With this heavy fire pouring into their flank and van, the Zulus wavered and made off back the way they had come. Barrow remounted his men to clear the scrub before pursuing up the right spur.

Officers of the garrison of Fort Pearson.

Natal Native Contingent of No. 1 Column. River Tugela in the background.

Camp of the 3rd Buffs at the Lower Tugela.

While the left horn was being repulsed, the rest of the impi appeared on the crest, some moving into the kraal while others headed for the left-hand spur. Lloyd switched his guns to fire on the kraal, under cover of which the sailors and Buffs advanced up the slope with the Gatling. Once the kraal was taken, the Gatling was moved on to the crest where its rapid fire soon drove the Zulus off the centre and left end of the ridge, as the mounted troops came up the right-hand spur to complete what had been a well-directed action. The Zulus had held the advantages of surprise and the high ground, while the column had been spread out and at rest. Pearson, however, had wrested the initiative from them and put in a successful counter-attack for the loss of ten men killed and sixteen wounded. It was a promising start on a day when 60 miles to the north-west No. 3 Column was within hours of total disaster.

Having lost 350 killed the impi withdrew, leaving Pearson free to continue his march unhindered, reaching Eshowe 2,000 feet above sea level on the following day. Welman's division marched in on the 24th, having encountered no Zulus. The only buildings at Eshowe were the deserted church, school and house of a Norwegian missionary. A quarter of a mile away low hills surrounded it on the north, east and west, but to the south a ridge afforded a distant view of the Indian Ocean and Fort Pearson on the Tugela some 30 miles away. On the 25th Pearson sent back a convoy of empty wagons, escorted by two companies each of the Buffs and 99th, to collect fresh supplies from the Lower Drift, while the rest of the troops began digging an entrenchment around the mission.

The next day Pearson received two messages from the Lower Drift which caused him some concern. The first said that Fort Tenedos had been attacked the previous night but had beaten off the Zulus. The second, which had been telegraphed by Sir Bartle Frere from Pietermaritzburg, said that Durnford's No. 2 Column had been wiped out. As far as Pearson knew, Durnford was at Middle Drift, which meant that the wagons he had sent back and his posts at Lower Drift could be in grave danger. If the latter fell, he would be cut off from Natal and the road to Pietermaritzburg and Durban would be open to a Zulu invasion.

On the 28th, six days after Isandhlwana, Pearson heard from Chelmsford. Without giving any details of the fate of the centre column,

Chelmsford informed him that all previous orders were cancelled, and that he was to take such action as he thought fit to preserve his column, including withdrawal from Eshowe if necessary. If he withdrew he was to try to hold on to the bridgehead at the Lower Drift, but he might be attacked by the whole Zulu Army.

Without any precise information as to the whereabouts of the enemy, it was difficult for Pearson to know what to do for the best. Although his fortifications around the mission would soon be complete, it was not ideal for defence in view of the hills and thick cover in the immediate vicinity. He was all right for ammunition but there were insufficient supplies to maintain the force he had at Eshowe for long. The general consensus of his subordinates, whom he consulted, was for withdrawal back to the Lower Drift, but when news suddenly came in that the wagons were returning with five companies of the 99th and N.N.C. this decision was reversed. To reduce the number of mouths to feed, Pearson sent back Barrow with all the mounted troops and most of the 2nd N.N.C. on the 29th, followed on the next day by 1,200 draught oxen, for which there was no grazing, escorted by the last of the N.N.C. The latter had hardly left Eshowe before they were attacked by Zulus, whereupon they fled back to the fort, leaving 900 of the precious oxen in enemy hands.

The fort which had been constructed to enclose the mission was roughly rectangular, 200 yards long and 50 wide, with loopholed walls 6 feet high, and was surrounded by a broad ditch in which sharpened stakes were embedded. The wagons were laagered inside the walls, thus forming a second line of defence should the outer rampart fall, and providing shelter for the troops who bivouacked underneath. The six remaining companies of the Buffs were allotted alarm posts on the long north and shorter west walls; the three of the 99th held the south; and the east was the responsibility of the sailors and sappers. A horse and cattle kraal was constructed, thorn

Sailors manning a Gatling gun on top of Fort Pearson. The seaman in the centre holds a fresh magazine. Note the white cap covers and cutlasses worn by the men.

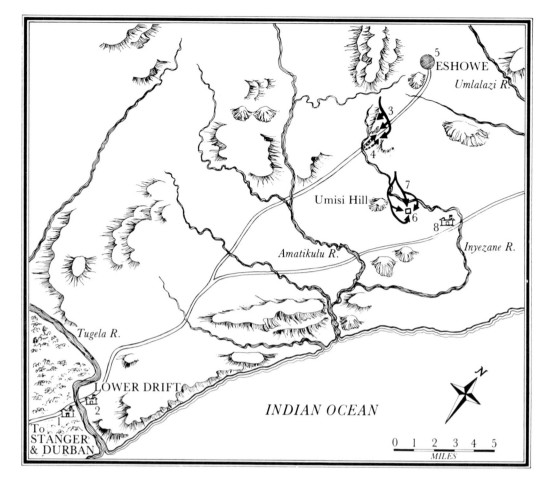

Operations at Eshowe and Gingindhlovu.

bushes and branches made an abattis, and a field of fire was cleared all round out to 800 yards, with the different ranges marked by posts. The garrison numbered 1,300 soldiers and sailors, plus the 400 wagoners.

On 2 February large bodies of Zulus appeared on the surrounding hills. Although they retreated when shelled by the 7-pounders, the sight of their numbers impelled Pearson to send off a request for reinforcements. Just over

a week later he learned for the first time the full extent of the centre column's defeat; he was also told that no reinforcements could be made available and that he was now entirely on his own, but that he could still withdraw if this was feasible. Reluctant to abandon the position but concerned about how long his supplies would last and the effect of the damp weather on his men's health, he suggested sending back part of the garrison, if Chelmsford agreed. No reply

84

Troops of the 99th Regiment about to cross the Tugela in a pont.

Fort Tenedos on the Zulu bank of the Tugela.

was received to this message, and as no further runners arrived in the ensuing days it became clear that they were now cut off in Eshowe.

As February dragged by, the Zulus, though always evident, made no attempt to attack but contented themselves with sniping at the fort and skirmishing with Pearson's patrols. The troops passed the time improving their defences, playing games, or listening to the bands of the Buffs and 99th. Although the ration scale was reduced, the men remained cheerful but, without proper protection from the continual rain and fog at nights, numbers began to go down with fever and dysentery, and the improvised hospital in the mission church was soon full.

At the beginning of March, as a diversion, Pearson led a raid to burn one of Dabulamanzi's kraals 7 miles away. The next day the sun came out and everyone's spirits were raised when a heliograph was spotted signalling from Fort Pearson. A makeshift apparatus was rigged up to reply, and over the next few days the garrison learned that a relief force would leave the Lower Drift on 13 March and that they were to advance to meet it on the Inyezane. This was cheering news indeed, for the rations, though not yet exhausted, were now deficient of many commodities, the meat issue had become dependent on slaughtering draught oxen, which made for tough chewing, and

sickness was taking an increasing toll with more than twenty dead and several critically ill. Then, a few days later, the heliograph flashed out the news that it had been necessary to postpone the attempt until 1 April.

While No. 1 Column had, through no fault of its own, been shut up in Eshowe, Chelmsford had been trying to pick up the pieces of his now ruined grand design for the conquest of Zululand. Leaving Rorke's Drift on 23 January he rode via Helpmakaar and Ladysmith back to Pietermaritzburg where he found the news of Isandhlwana had preceded him, setting the capital in a flurry of nervous anticipation and preparations to withstand a Zulu descent on the town.

So comprehensive and resolute were the measures taken by Lieutenant-Colonel Mitchell of the Royal Marine Light Infantry to turn Pietermaritzburg into a fortress that, far from allaying the fears of the civilian population, the barricades and sand-bagged houses merely convinced them that Cetshwayo's warriors would be rampaging down the street at any minute. Although neither they nor the military had any means of knowing it, they stood in no danger whatever. Not only had Cetshwayo forbidden any invasion of Natal but the impi that had attacked at Isandhlwana and Rorke's Drift had returned to their home kraals, as was their custom after a battle.

No. 1 Column's completed camp on the Zulu bank of the Tugela.

Wagons crossing the Amatikulu Drift on the way to Eshowe. One of the Royal Engineers is supervising operations in the foreground.

Chelmsford could then only send off the uninformative message that Pearson received on 28 January, while a similar order went to Evelyn Wood, commanding the left column, who had already heard the news of Isandhlwana from another source. He then drew up his despatch for the Colonial Secretary in London, informing him that no further action could be taken until he had received reinforcements to make good the losses of the battle of the 22nd. The next matter that engaged his attention was the Court of Inquiry he had convened to inquire into the defeat. The Court took evidence from those survivors who were readily available but, since it was not required to do so, submitted no opinion as to responsibility for it. In general conversation around Pietermaritzburg, however, it soon emerged that most people, some with knowledge of the events and a good few without, were laying the blame on Durnford who, it was claimed, as the senior officer at Isandhlwana should never have left the camp, thus splitting the force mustered for its defence. Durnford's admiration for the Africans, his criticism of the Natal Volunteers on a previous expedition, and his liaison with the daughter of the Bishop of Natal, despite being long estranged from his own wife, had earned him many enemies in colonial society so that, in the prevailing mood of panic that seized the colony, an unpopular dead man made a ready scapegoat. Chelmsford himself forbore from apportioning blame and waited to hear from London.

At Cape Town the authorities prepared to send the last three companies of the 2/4th King's Own and part of the 88th up to Natal. As the news of Isandhlwana was flashed to

A Colonial volunteer on vedette duty. Engraving from the Illustrated London News.

London, the captain of H.M.S. *Shah*, then sailing for home, heard it at St. Helena. Promptly embarking a further company of the 88th and a section of 8/7 Battery R.A. from the garrison, he set course for Durban. At home the tragedy created a wave of horror among the general public, which seldom showed any concern for its soldiers in peacetime, as sober Victorian families took in the full measure of the massacre of their brave men by hordes of savages, so graphically displayed in the popular press. (Since only one correspondent, the ex-officer C. L. Norris-Newman, had been present with No. 3 Column, his paper, the *Standard*, obtained a scoop and the imagination of many other journalists had to work at full stretch.) For the Government the news could not have come at a worse time. Bartle Frere's high-handed policy towards Zululand had been bad enough, but the Prime Minister, Disraeli,

already preoccupied with the Afghan War and the danger of conflict with Russia, had regarded it as a purely colonial problem and left Hicks Beach to deal with it. Now Frere's machinations had led to a serious and expensive reverse which was bound to result in a political storm at the most inconvenient moment. Afghanistan was undoubtedly the more serious issue, but since the Zulu business had been started it had better be finished quickly. Although Chelmsford had only asked for three battalions to replace the 1/24th and the two of the 3rd N.N.C., within five days of the Government's receiving the news on 11 February substantial reinforcements of nearly 10,500 men and over 1,800 horses were under orders for Natal: two cavalry regiments, five infantry battalions from home and one from Ceylon, three batteries, and detachments of the administrative services in proportion, as well as

The officers of H.M.S. Active. *Second from the left in front is Midshipman Coker, who commanded the Gatling at the fight on the Inyezane. He later died at Eshowe.*

An eyewitness sketch of the 3rd Buffs and Naval Brigade in action on the Inyezane, 22 January.

drafts to make good the losses of units already in South Africa. By the end of February the crowded transports were pulling out into the Channel.

With the attention of the public now focused on Zululand, newspaper editors despatched urgent telegrams to their experienced war correspondents and artists, many of whom had either been covering the Russo-Turkish War in the Balkans or the events in Afghanistan. From far and wide they headed post-haste for Durban, determined that Victorian breakfast tables should not be denied one iota of the dramatic incidents soon to unfold in distant Natal: the ex-cavalry trooper, Archibald Forbes, of the *Daily News*, Francis of *The Times*, Melton Prior of the *Illustrated London News* and Charles Fripp of the *Graphic*, from whose brush would later appear the huge, dramatic, but not wholly accurate canvas of the 24th's last stand at Isandhlwana. Rivalling his artistic interpretations of the war would be the talents of the celebrated French battle painter, Alphonse de Neuville. The corpses scattered round Isandhlwana and the valiant defenders of Rorke's Drift had turned a minor colonial punitive expedition into a major campaign.

On the day before the despatches reached London, Chelmsford had ridden up to the Lower Drift to examine the possibilities of relieving Pearson in Eshowe, but he at once appreciated that nothing could be done until the reinforcements arrived from England. He therefore returned to Pietermaritzburg to reorganize the native troops and volunteers, and to rebuild his transport train.

The remains of the ill-fated 3rd N.N.C. were disbanded, the European elements being drafted to form a squadron of Natal Horse. The three battalions of the 1st and the two of the 2nd N.N.C. were reconstituted into five independent battalions with a higher proportion of rifles than before. The Natal Native Horse went back to recruit in their tribal areas, and fresh units of Volunteers came in from Cape Colony and the Transvaal.

On 6 March H.M.S. *Shah* arrived with her embarked troops from St Helena, followed in quick succession by the 57th Regiment from Ceylon, the 91st Highlanders – one of three Highland regiments which wore trews instead of the kilt – and the green-clad 3/60th Rifles. H.M.S. *Boadicea* disembarked a landing party of 228 which, added to those from the *Shah*, swelled the Naval Brigade to nearly 900 men. With these fresh troops Chelmsford was ready to march to Pearson's relief. Taking command of the column in person he began the advance from Fort Tenedos on 29 March. To assist his progress he requested Evelyn Wood, still far in the north with No. 4 Column, to create a diversion in that area.

The column was formed in two divisions. The Advance Division, under Lieutenant-Colonel Law, R.A., comprised 350 of the Naval Brigade, the balance of the two regiments in Eshowe (two companies of the Buffs and five of the 99th), the 91st Highlanders and the 4th N.N.C. Battalion. The Rear Division was under the command of Lieutenant-Colonel Leigh Pemberton of the 3/60th, who had six companies of his own battalion, 190 Naval Brigade, a company of Royal Marine Light Infantry, the 57th and the 5th N.N.C. Battalion. The column artillery, manned entirely by the Royal Navy and Royal Marines, had two 9-pounders, four 24-pounder rocket tubes and two Gatlings. Major Barrow again commanded the mounted troops, which numbered 400, divided between 120 Europeans from the

Mounted Infantry and a new unit called the Natal Volunteer Guides, 130 of the Natal Native Horse, and 150 scouts raised by John Dunn, the so-called 'White Zulu' who had borne the news of Frere's ultimatum to Cetshwayo. In all, Chelmsford had a force of 3,390 Europeans and 2,280 Africans.

Infantry signallers with a heliograph.

The north-east fortifications of Eshowe. A photograph taken after its evacuation.

Departure of the reinforcements from England. The 17th Lancers leaving Victoria Dock, Black-wall. An engraving from the Illustrated London News.

Victoria Military Hospital on the Natal side of the Lower Tugela. Fort Pearson beyond to the left.

The officers of the 91st Highlanders. Note the tartan trews worn by this regiment and the Highland version of the undress serge frock. The tall young officer in the centre of the back row wears the full dress doublet.

To avoid the possibility of an ambush in the close country through which Pearson had passed, Chelmsford followed another track along the coast for the first few days. He nevertheless still had to cross the transverse rivers, which were flooded by heavy rains, and since he was determined not to risk any repetition of Isandhlwana much time was taken laagering and entrenching the camp at the end of each day's march. Progress was therefore slow, but by the evening of 1 April, Pearson's observers in Eshowe could see the relief column moving into laager on the south bank of the Inyezane, near the kraal of Gingindhlovu which No. 1 Column had burned exactly ten weeks before. With luck, the following day should see the end of their long incarceration, which by now was imposing quite severe hardships of hunger, exposure and sickness.

The laager was sited on a 300-foot ridge running roughly west-east, just over 1,000 yards south-east of a bend in the Inyezane where it bore off in a north-easterly direction. West of the ridge the ground dipped, only to rise again to the 470-foot high Umisi Hill, the summit of which was a mile and a quarter south-west of the laager, and just under three-quarters of a mile due south of the nearest loop of the Inyezane. In all other directions the ground sloped away, giving a good field of fire all round the laager. There were 120 wagons lined up diagonally to each other and lashed together to form a square with sides of 130 yards in length. A trench was dug 20 yards outside the wagons, using the earth to build a waist-high wall between it and the vehicles. Within the wagon laager were situated Barrow's mounted troops, the N.N.C., 3,000 cattle and the spare transport.

The infantry bivouacked in the 20-yard space between the wagons and the wall so that they could instantly man their battle

Men of the 57th Regiment entrenching a laager. A drawing for the Graphic *by Charles Fripp.*

stations. Holding the front or north-west face nearest the Inyezane were the 57th with a Gatling on either flank in the corners of the square. The rear face was allotted to the seven companies of the Buffs and 99th, with the two 9-pounders on their left flank and the rockets on their right in the two rear corners. The left or south-west face was held by the 60th, leaving the fourth side to the 91st.

While the laager was being constructed and the men were cooking their evening meal, Barrow's scouts rode in to report that the Zulus were massing on the far side of Umisi Hill. John Dunn decided to verify this report by scouting along the river bank under cover of a heavy rainstorm and the approaching darkness. He returned after night had fallen with the news that there were no Zulus south of the river but that an impi was camped on the far bank, north-west of the laager.

Darkness had prevented Dunn from assessing the Zulu strength, but there were in

Zulu prisoners taken at Gingindhlovu guarded by troops, probably of the 3rd Buffs.

fact 12,000 of them: the uVe, inGobamakhosi, umCijo and elements of the umHlanga, umBonambi and uThulwane. They were thus all regiments that had been at Isandhlwana, but some of them had recently endured a less auspicious encounter as a result of

The field of Gingindhlovu with skeletons of Zulu dead.

The 91st Highlanders in Zululand. The Pioneer Sergeant and three pioneers are in front, followed by the Drum-Major with behind him four pipers, who alone of this regiment wore the kilt. Between the pipers and the leading company are the drummers. This regiment had black leather pouches instead of buff and are carrying their greatcoats rolled instead of folded on their backs. The companies are formed in quarter column.

Chelmsford's order to Wood to create a diversion, as will be seen shortly. The force on the Inyezane was commanded by Somopo, whom Cetshwayo had told to prevent the relief column linking up with Eshowe. Cetshwayo had been appalled at the losses suffered by his army hitherto and had warned Somopo to incur as few casualties as possible. Somopo had intended to ambush the column while it crossed one of the drifts on the inner track, as the Zulus had tried to do to Pearson, but Chelmsford's taking the coastal route had thwarted this plan. With the column now within a day's march of Eshowe and with only the Inyezane to cross, Somopo had but one chance left.

With the rain falling steadily and the mass of men and animals churning the confined space of the laager into a quagmire, added to a certain apprehension since the majority of the troops had never even seen a Zulu, the column spent an uneasy night. Nothing, however, disturbed their restless sleep, and it must be assumed that Cetshwayo's earlier admonitions against night attacks were still in force.

Dawn on 2 April broke in a thick mist. Realizing that he could not move his wagons before the ground dried out, Chelmsford decided to remain in laager and send out the N.N.C. to try to provoke the enemy into attacking while he still held a strong position. While the troops were still manning the walls for the dawn 'stand-to', however, the outlying picquets came in to report that the impi was advancing eastwards. The mist cleared rapidly to reveal the Zulu left horn running along the north bank, then swinging right to cross the river in two columns. One of the Gatlings fired a long burst before the Zulus disappeared into the tall grass on the south bank before re-emerging in three groups. The chest and right horn came over the northern slopes of Umisi Hill, each also in three groups, and the whole charging buffalo formation closed in at a run on three sides of the laager. The infantry opened fire at between 300 and 400 yards, the crash of their volleys adding to the rattle of the Gatlings and the shriek of the rockets. This was the type of battle that Chelmsford had always envisaged as the decisive counter to the speed and ferocity of the enveloping Zulu charge. The fire of some enemy marksmen caused a few casualties within the laager, but these were nothing compared to the heaps of black warriors falling in front of the flashing rifle and Gatling barrels. Though the Zulu regiments made persistent rushes to get within stabbing range, their charges lacked the drive and spirit that had impelled them forward at Isandhlwana and Rorke's Drift. After twenty minutes, with their dense ranks riven by the volleys, the heart went out of the attack and the entire impi began to crumble away. Seeing them waver, Chelmsford launched Barrow in a charge, followed by the N.N.C. By 7.30 a.m. it was all over, and the Zulus had fled beyond the Inyezane or the Umisi Hill. No group of warriors had got nearer than 20 yards from the square.

The bodies counted round the laager totalled 700 and some 300 more were despatched during the pursuit. Fatal casualties in the column included Lieutenant-Colonel Northey (who had commanded the 3/60th since Leigh Pemberton had been appointed to the Rear Division), an officer of the 99th, one private of the Buffs, one of the 60th, three of the 91st and five of the N.N.C.; a further forty-eight had been wounded.

Up at Eshowe, Pearson had been ready to sally out with his garrison as instructed a month before. After he had seen the early defeat of the impi he decided to remain where he was, since it would take him four hours to reach the Inyezane. With Pearson no longer in danger, Chelmsford devoted the rest of the day to clearing up after the battle and preparing for the steep climb up to Eshowe. On 3 April the troops marched in, led, in the seemingly traditional style of all relief columns, by the 91st Highlanders with pipers playing and Colours flying, to be greeted with cheers and some emotion by the garrison, thankful that its two-month blockade was over.

Ruins of the mission house at Eshowe after it had been burned.

A pontoon bridge constructed over the Lower Tugela.

Chelmsford concluded that no purpose would be served by retaining Eshowe, so the laboriously constructed defences were demolished. Pearson's men set off for the Lower Drift on the 4th, Chelmsford following on the next day after a fruitless attempt by a mounted patrol to capture Dabulamanzi, who had been reported recuperating after Gingindhlovu in his kraal 6 miles away. Pearson followed his original route while Chelmsford swung off on to the coastal track. As they bivouacked on the first night, they could see that Eshowe had been set alight by the Zulus. On nearing the coast Chelmsford detached Leigh Pemberton's division with orders to construct a new advanced base on the south bank of the Inyezane, 16 miles up the coastal track from the Lower Drift. It was called Fort Chelmsford. By the 12th, Law's division and all Pearson's column were back in Natal.

In the three months since the invasion began Cetshwayo's spear-and-shield army had destroyed one column and rendered a second ineffective. With the decisive victory of Gingindhlovu under his belt, however, and with more reinforcements arriving at Durban, Chelmsford's confidence in a successful outcome of the war grew. This he badly needed, for, although the last of his original columns had not suffered the disaster of No. 3, nor the misfortunes of No. 1, the operations in the north had not been without their losses and setbacks.

7

Hlobane and Kambula

Advancing from Utrecht, Colonel Evelyn Wood's No. 4 Column had crossed the Blood River on 10 January and moved south to support Chelmsford's crossing of the Buffalo on the 11th. Since, as has been seen, the latter was unopposed, no action was necessary, but during the day Wood conferred with Chelmsford who had ridden north to meet him. Rising from the plains of north-west Zululand was a series of flat-topped mountains wherein dwelt a number of tribes whose distance from Ulundi gave them a measure of independence from Cetshwayo's rule. This had enabled their chiefs to withhold their warriors for local defence, rather than contributing to the main Zulu Army. Chelmsford required Wood to occupy the attentions of these tribes so that they would not interfere with the operations of No. 3 Column during its advance to Isandhlwana and thence to Ulundi.

Wood established a camp at Bemba's Kop on the east bank of the Blood River, spending five days there in pouring rain while he sent his mounted Colonials and Boers under Lieutenant-Colonel Buller out to a radius of 40 miles or more, scouring the country to the east. Redvers Buller had been commissioned in 1858 in the 60th Rifles and, after seeing service with his regiment in the China War of 1860, had attracted Wolseley's attention during the latter's Red River Expedition in 1870, becoming his head of Intelligence during the Ashanti War three years later. He was a big, muscular man of great strength and endurance, which, added to his total fearlessness and drive, endowed him with outstanding powers of leadership. The results he achieved with the Frontier Light Horse during the Kaffir War and Sekukuni's rebellion had demonstrated a knack with the independently-minded colonials of which few Imperial officers were capable. In his later career serious defects in this seemingly impregnable character were to appear, but in 1879, as the commander of Wood's mounted force, he was in his element. Together, he and Wood, of whom it was said that 'few understand savage warfare better', were a formidable combination.

Between 12 and 16 January, Buller and his troopers patrolled ceaselessly across northern Zululand, but though they brought in numerous cattle they saw no major concentrations of Zulus. On the 17th, therefore, Wood advanced his whole column north-eastwards, and by the 20th had established a laager at Tinta's kraal on the White Umfolozi. Some 10 miles north of the kraal a chain of flat-topped mountains, Zunguin, Hlobane and Ityentika, each connected by a nek, ran for 15 miles in a north-easterly direction. While Wood's infantry fortified the new camp, Buller rode out to investigate these mountains but was attacked from Zunguin by 1,000 Zulus of the abaQulusi. He drew off, sending back a report to Wood

Exterior of the military laager at Utrecht.

who joined him with most of the 1/13th and 90th before dawn on the 21st. An attack was mounted on the Zunguin from where the Zulus fled back to Hlobane, on top of which, during the afternoon, Wood could see some 4,000 Zulus drilling.

On the 22nd, the day of Isandhlwana, and on the day following, Wood rested his men in preparation for an advance against the heights at dawn on the 24th. After some skirmishing during the morning, Wood had halted for lunch below the western slopes of Hlobane, when a messenger arrived with news of the disaster to the centre column. Wood immediately appreciated that he was now operating in the air. After falling back to Tinta's kraal, he decided, in view of the kraal's unsuitability for a long stay, to move his base north-westwards to Kambula Hill, about 14 miles due west of Zunguin, from where he could cover the approaches to Utrecht and Luneburg at the same time as keeping an eye on the Zulus around Hlobane. By the 31st he was in his new position where he received his first communication from Chelmsford since their meeting on the 11th. This message, very similar to the one received on the 28th by Pearson at Eshowe, told him that he was now on his own,

that he could expect no reinforcements, and that he must be prepared to have the whole Zulu Army upon him.

Despite the collapse of the initial over-all plan, Wood had no intention of remaining idle until the offensive could be resumed. He determined to capitalize on the near-autonomy of the northern tribes by trying to wean them from any allegiance they felt towards Cetshwayo, centring his hopes on Uhamu, Cetshwayo's half-brother, who had always been friendly towards the British and at odds with the King. In addition, he planned to give assistance to Colonel Rowlands' No. 5 Column, based on Luneburg, who was being plagued by marauding bands of Zulus raiding across the eastern Transvaal border. The burden of these manoeuvres fell upon Buller and the mounted troops, who day after day throughout February rode out from Kambula with tireless energy, raiding the outlying kraals, seizing their cattle to will the inhabitants into submission, searching for Uhamu who had gone into hiding, or riding north to attack the marauders on the border.

At Kambula, Wood took up a position on a ridge and set his infantry to construct a hexagonal laager with the wagons locked tightly together, and a separate kraal for the cattle 200 yards to the south-east on the edge of the southern face of the ridge. Both were surrounded by trenches and earth parapets, and a stone-built redoubt was sited on a rise just north of the kraal. The hundred yards or so between the kraal and the redoubt were blocked by a palisade, while four 7-pounders of 11/7 R.A. were positioned in the gap between the redoubt and the laager, covering the northern approaches, and two more guns were placed in the redoubt facing north-east.

Here he received much-needed reinforcements of mounted men, Lieutenant-Colonel Russell's squadron of Mounted Infantry and the re-formed Edendale troop of Natal Native Horse. From the Transvaal, there arrived two troops of Commandant Raaf's Transvaal Rangers and a troop of the Border Horse raised by Commandant Weatherley, a settler of Canadian origins who had been a cavalry officer in the Crimean War and the Sepoy Mutiny, but who had left the Army in doubtful circumstances and had just divorced his wife. In late February rumours of potential trouble brewing among the Transvaal Boers required Colonel Rowlands to remove to Pretoria, turning No. 5 Column over to Wood's command. The troop of German settlers forming the Kaffrarian Vanguard at Luneburg rode down to Kambula, and Wood's regular infantry battalions were now increased by Major Tucker's five companies of the 80th Regiment, also at Luneburg. Although this regiment had been in South Africa since 1876 and had been engaged against Sekukuni, it had so far seen nothing of the war. It was about to encounter its realities in earnest.

Colonel Evelyn Wood of No. 4 Column in the field. Water colour by Lt-Col. J. N. Crealock.

The garrison at Luneburg was supplied by periodic convoys despatched from Lydenburg, 160 miles to the north in the Transvaal. In late February one such convoy of twenty wagons containing ammunition and rations left Lydenburg but, owing to the bad state of the roads after the heavy rains, had suffered numerous breakdowns and delays along the road. It had finally been halted by flooding 6 miles away at Myer's Drift over the Intombi River.

On 7 March, Tucker sent out Captain Moriarty's H Company with a wagon-load of materials for building a raft to bring the convoy in. When Moriarty reached the Intombi, he found that one wagon which had been bogged down in the drift had been pulled out, but that a further six on the far, north bank were unable to cross as the river was in spate. Having constructed a raft, and leaving a subaltern with thirty-four men on the south bank, Moriarty crossed the river on the following day with the rest of his company. He left a few men to prepare a camp and marched north to search for the remaining wagons. He found them halted some 3 miles away, having lost forty-six of their draught oxen to a raid by marauders. By using the remaining oxen in relays, he got them all down to the north bank of the Intombi on the 9th. The rain set in again, however, making any crossing impossible; so he formed a V-shaped laager on the north bank with the open end on the river.

The rain continued without ceasing until the afternoon of the 11th when Tucker rode up from Luneburg to see what was happening. He did not think much of Moriarty's laager, for the wagons were not locked up tightly with their poles run under one another, and there were gaps between the end wagons of the V and the river, owing to the water having fallen slightly since they were pushed into place. Tucker was 'an outstandingly fit and strong-minded officer' but, appreciating Moriarty's difficulties in manoeuvring the wagons into position owing to the state of the ground, he did not press the

Lieutenant-Colonel Redvers Buller, 60th Rifles, commanding the mounted troops of No. 4 Column. Water colour by Lt-Col. J. N. Crealock.

point; in any case Moriarty hoped to get the wagons across on the next day and the possibilities of an enemy attack so close to Luneburg seemed remote. Tucker rode home leaving Moriarty to make his own arrangements for the night.

Shoeing Buller's horses at a field forge, No. 4 Column.

Commissariat staff and wagons of the 90th Light Infantry.

103

Despite the thick bush surrounding the area, Moriarty posted no outlying picquets, contenting himself with single sentries on either side of the laager. His subaltern, Lieutenant Harward, had been out with a few men during the afternoon to search for some strayed cattle, and returning late and tired had laid down to sleep in Moriarty's tent. As there was only an N.C.O., Colour-Sergeant Booth, with the 34-strong detachment on the south bank, Moriarty made Harward cross onto that side.

At 3.30 a.m., when the rain had started again and thick mist covered the river, one of Harward's sentries heard a shot to the north. Harward stood his men to and sent a message across the river to warn Moriarty, but the latter, after warning his sentries to be on the alert, went back to sleep. At first light around 5 a.m., with the mist clearing, the sentry on the south bank suddenly saw a body of about 800 Zulus encircling the wagon laager. He fired his rifle and raised the alarm, which was taken up by the sentries on the north bank. The troops immediately turned out, but before they could man their alarm posts the Zulus were into the laager, stabbing at the sleepy men as they stumbled from their tents. Moriarty himself had rushed from his tent outside the laager as soon as he heard the alarm, but found himself surrounded. He shot three of the enemy but fell mortally wounded by assegais as he tried to clamber over the wagons, crying out: 'I'm done for. Fire away, boys! Death or glory!' Within a few moments all the eighty-odd soldiers and wagoners in the laager had been killed, except for twelve who managed to throw themselves into the river.

On the south bank Harward's detachment had opened fire across the river, but a party of 200 Zulus crossed higher upstream and advanced rapidly to attack and cut off their retreat. Harward's formation was quickly broken up, and telling Colour-Sergeant Booth to fall back to a farmhouse 3,000 yards away he galloped off to Luneburg to fetch help. Booth managed to assemble Lance-Corporal Burgess

1st Battalion, 13th Light Infantry, on the march in Zululand accompanied by scouts of the Natal Native Horse. Water colour by Orlando Norie.

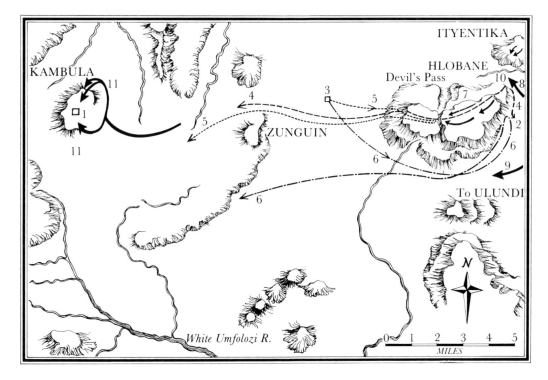

Operations at Hlobane and Kambula.

and ten men and retreated steadily in a formed body, holding the Zulus off with volleys. Some other survivors joined him, but four men who broke away from the party were all killed.

At about 6.30 a.m. Harward broke in on Tucker with the news of the attack. Tucker immediately mounted as many men as he could find horses for and rode hard for the Intombi, ordering another 150 to follow on. He came up with Booth, who had reached safety with his group at the farmhouse, but on approaching the river he could see the Zulus making off eastwards, having looted the wagons. A single soldier and two Kaffirs emerged from hiding but all the rest of Moriarty's command were dead.

Out of a strength of 106, 62 had been killed or were missing, and a further 17 of the wagoners were also slain.

For his brave and steady conduct during his withdrawal, Colour-Sergeant Booth was subsequently awarded the Victoria Cross. When a report of the affair reached Chelmsford, he was furious at the negligence of precautions it disclosed and at the conduct of Harward. Moriarty was beyond his wrath, but he ordered Harward to be tried by general court martial for abandoning his men in the face of the enemy and for failing to ensure the safety of his camp. At his trial the following February (1880), Harward insisted that he could not have formed

Commandant Pieter Raaf of the Transvaal Rangers.

a laager with the only two wagons he had had on the south bank; that his precautions had given earlier warning than Moriarty's; and that, once the defence collapsed, aid had to be summoned, and since he was the only man with a horse he had done so. The court acquitted him on both counts, but when its findings came up for review by Sir Garnet Wolseley, by then commanding in Natal, he refused to confirm them, maintaining that the acquittal had been based on 'a monstrous theory, viz., that a regimental officer who is the only officer present with a party of soldiers actually and seriously engaged with the enemy, can, under any pretext whatever, be justified in deserting them, and by so doing, abandoning them to their fate. The more helpless a position in which an officer finds his men, the more it is his bounden duty to stay and share their fortune, whether for good or ill.' Harward returned to duty, but the Commander-in-Chief of the Army, the Duke of Cambridge, endorsed Wolseley's remarks and ordered them to be read out to every regiment in the service.

Three days before news of the blow to the 80th reached Wood on 13 March, Uhamu had come into the camp at Kambula with 700 of his tribe to request assistance in bringing out the rest of his people from their hiding-places in caves near the headwaters of the Black Umfolozi. This sort of defection was one of the things Wood had been striving for, but the area was 50 miles to the east and only 40 from Ulundi, so that the prospect of searching for and escorting to safety large numbers, which would include women, children and the elderly, held considerable risks. Nevertheless he decided it was worth it and set out on the 14th with 360 of Buller's mounted men and 200 of Uhamu's warriors. Two days later, although some of Uhamu's people had been lost to attacks by Zulus loyal to Cetshwayo, Wood and Buller returned to Kambula with over 900 refugees.

Shortly after this coup, Wood received Chelmsford's request to create a diversion in the north, which Chelmsford hoped would draw off some of the Zulu strength while he attempted to relieve Eshowe. Wood had already heard reports of an impi preparing to leave Ulundi on 26 March for an attack on either Kambula or Utrecht. He knew that the abaQulusi on Hlobane had been reinforced by some of the main Zulu army, but he reckoned that, by attacking Hlobane on 28 March before the impi could reach the area, he could drive off the cattle on the mountain, which would induce the impi to attack him in his well-prepared position at Kambula.

Hlobane consisted of two plateaux, the lower and smaller of which rose to a height of about 850 feet at the eastern end of the 4-mile-long nek connecting it to the Zunguin to its south-west. At its eastern end the lower plateau terminated in a point, before rising very steeply for another 200 feet up a narrow, boulder-strewn way forming a series of giant steps, known as the Devil's Pass, to the higher plateau, roughly $3\frac{1}{2}$ miles long by $1\frac{1}{2}$ wide. The eastern slopes fell to a terrace and thence to the Ityentika nek, leading to the mountain of the same name. The sides of both plateaux were very steep, if not sheer, and there were only two tracks up to the summits: one, almost impassable to horses, led up a salient at the western end; the other ran up the angle of a re-entrant near the eastern end. On the top there were some 2,000 head of cattle and about 1,000 Zulus, many of whom had firearms.

Field kitchen of the 80th Regiment. Note the bowler hat worn instead of a helmet.

107

The attack on the 80th Regiment at the Intombi River Drift. An engraving from the Illustrated London News.

Wood's plan was for Buller to scale the eastern track up to the higher plateau with 359 of the Frontier Light Horse, Baker's Horse, Transvaal Rangers and Border Horse, 32 of Uys' burghers, a rocket trough of 11/7 R.A. and the 2nd Battalion of friendly Zulus; once on top he was to drive off the cattle. Russell was to take the western track and occupy the lower plateau with the Mounted Infantry, Kaffrarian Vanguard, Natal Native Horse, the second rocket trough and the other battalion of friendlies. Wood himself was to direct operations with his principal staff officer, Captain Hon. R. Campbell, Coldstream

Mbilini (right) who led the attack on the 80th at the Intombi River.

Guards, his A.D.C., Lieutenant Lysons, 90th, his political agent, Mr Lloyd, and an escort of eight mounted infantrymen of the 90th and seven mounted Zulus.

After leaving Kambula at dawn on the 27th, Buller bivouacked that evening 5 miles southeast of Hlobane, while Russell took up position some 3 miles to the west of the mountain, where he was joined by Wood. Somehow Weatherley's Border Horse had become detached from Buller, but he could not wait for them. At 10 p.m., leaving his bivouac fires blazing to deceive any watchers on Hlobane, he moved to the Ityentika nek. At 3.30 a.m., gravely hampered by an appalling thunderstorm, his troopers began the hazardous ascent, leading their horses. The lightning flashes revealed their progress to Zulus in the caves above, who opened fire, causing some casualties, chiefly to horses, but

Captain D. Moriarty, 80th Regiment, who lost his life during the Zulu attack on his company at the Intombi River Drift.

by 6 a.m. the storm had passed and Buller reached the summit. He found that some of the abaQulusi had moved to the far, eastern end of the plateau, ready to cut him off from his line of retreat. Posting one troop of the Frontier Light Horse to hold them off, he set his native infantry to herding the cattle westwards, followed by the mounted men.

Russell meanwhile had been advancing up the lower plateau. Wood, moving east, encountered the missing Weatherley with his Border Horse. Hearing firing from the upper plateau, where the F.L.H. were engaging the abaQulusi, Wood ordered Weatherley to advance in that direction, but his men, chiefly English settlers from the Transvaal, refused. Wood rode on with his small party, intending to take Buller's path to the summit, and was eventually followed by the Border Horse. Coming under fire from some caves above, he missed the track and was confronted by a line of boulders. Mr Lloyd was killed and Wood ordered the Border Horse to clear the way; they again refused. Captain Campbell, Lysons and four of the escort went on alone against the nearest cave, but as Campbell charged in he was shot dead. Lysons and Private Fowler rushed forward and overcame the resistance. Wood was greatly upset by Campbell's death and, although his party was still under fire, was determined to carry his body and Lloyd's down for proper burial. Bugler Walkinshaw, Wood's orderly, risked his life by going back under fire to fetch a prayer book from the wallet on the saddle of Wood's horse which had been shot. When the short ceremony had been completed, Wood moved back westwards to join Russell. Weatherley, who by now had found the right track, rode off with his recalcitrant troopers towards the summit.

Just before 10.30 Wood, having reached the plain, was riding along the southern flank of Hlobane when he suddenly spotted five huge columns of Zulus to the south-east. This was the main impi, which unbeknown to him had left Ulundi a day earlier than forecast, and was now only 3 miles away and coming on fast. Some were already breaking away towards the Ityentika nek which would effectively block Buller's line of retreat, and once they reached the western end Russell would be trapped also. Even if both detachments could be withdrawn from Hlobane, there would be need for a rapid retreat to Kambula before the Zulus could get there. Wood hurriedly sent a message with Lysons for Russell, telling him of the impi's approach and ordering him to get into position on Zunguin Nek.

In fact, both Buller and Russell, with the advantage of high ground, had already observed the impi; in Russell's case an hour and a half earlier, when he had sent a warning to Buller who was still on the higher plateau. Around 9 a.m. Buller had been reconnoitring the drop at the Devil's Pass between the two plateaux, which was invisible from the plain.

Colour-Sergeant A. Booth, 80th Regiment, awarded the Victoria Cross for his conduct during the retreat of the survivors from the Intombi River.

110

A field bakery of Evelyn Wood's column.

Evelyn Wood's bodyguard of mounted infantrymen of the 90th Light Infantry. They are wearing corduroy breeches with scarlet serge frocks and are armed with Swinburne-Henry carbines.

Cetshwayo's half-brother, Uhamu, whose people Evelyn Wood rescued from Zululand.

Deeming it an impracticable route down, he turned back east to descend by the way he had come up, sending Captain Barton on ahead with thirty of the F.L.H. to bury the casualties incurred during the ascent, and then return to Kambula along the southern flank of the mountain. Barton had ridden off to the eastern end of the plateau where he fell in with the Border Horse, and together the two groups began to descend. Buller spotted the impi at about 9.20 and, although it was still 5 miles off, realized that to take the eastern track was now out of the question, and that his whole force, including the captured cattle, would have to chance the perilous drop down the Devil's Pass. It was too late to stop Barton, so he sent a galloper after him, ordering him 'to retreat at once by his right' by which he meant the northern flank of Hlobane. Unfortunately Barton, who had not yet seen the impi when he received this message, took it as confirmation of the earlier order to move by the southern flank. Thus he and the Border Horse rode unwittingly straight into the impi's right horn as it advanced. Driven back to the Ityentika Nek, they were caught by other Zulus descending from that mountain, and both detachments were massacred.

Russell also misinterpreted the order he received from Wood, though with less disastrous results. When Lysons reached him, he had already brought his force down from the lower plateau to Zunguin Nek, ready to cover Buller's withdrawal, so that, after conferring with his officers, he decided that Wood meant another nek to the west of Zunguin and rode off there, 6 miles from Hlobane.

Thus by 11 a.m. Buller was alone on the mountain, with the impi coming on across the plain, and the abaQulusi, hitherto held in check, coming out to harass the dangerous withdrawal down the drop. He had already driven the captured cattle and their escorts over the rim, and now he had to get his nervous troopers and their frenzied horses down this aptly-named Devil's Pass under an ever-increasing fire and darting attacks by the abaQulusi. Confusion was inevitable. Casualties mounted, many of the horses slipped and fell to their deaths, but somehow, largely by dint of his towering personality and heroic leadership, it was managed. Piet Uys, the only Boer who had offered his services to the Army and who had rendered invaluable support and advice to Buller, lost his life going back to help his eldest son. Much gallantry was shown in rescuing the wounded and Buller himself was everywhere, spurring his men on, saving others who were cut

Piet Uys, the leader of the Boer burghers with No. 4 Column, with his four sons, the eldest of whom (right) he died trying to save at Hlobane.

113

Lieutenant Henry Lysons, 90th Light Infantry, who won the Victoria Cross at Hlobane. In this photograph he wears the staff uniform of an A.D.C.

Private E. J. Fowler, 90th Light Infantry, who won the Victoria Cross with Lysons at Hlobane. He is shown in the uniform of the 18th Royal Irish Regiment to which he transferred after the Zulu War.

Another Hlobane V.C.: Lieutenant E. S. Browne, 24th Regiment.

Officers of the 90th Light Infantry. The bearded officer in the centre looking down is Major R. M. Rogers, V.C., who won the Cross as a subaltern with the 44th Regiment in the China War of 1860 He commanded the 90th in the Zulu War in the absence of Evelyn Wood as column commander.

114

off and not leaving the plateau until all were clear. On reaching the plain so many horses had been lost that only by men riding pillion on the remaining animals was it possible to get clear and ride for Kambula. The survivors made their own way back, some, including Buller, not reaching the camp until after dark. He had no sooner ridden in than he was told that a few remnants of Barton's force were lost about 8 miles away. Despite the exertions and strains of the last thirty-six hours he immediately rode out to look for them.

For his conspicuous gallantry and leadership at Hlobane, Buller later received the Victoria Cross. It also went to Lysons and Fowler, both of the 90th, for their dash into the cave, and to Major Knox Leet, of the 13th but commanding the friendly Zulus, and Lieutenant Browne, 24th, for going back to save the lives of wounded men during the descent of the Devil's Pass. Lieutenant D'Arcy of the Frontier Light Horse was also recommended by Wood for similar acts, but as a colonial he was deemed ineligible. This distinction would later be rectified.

Fifteen officers and seventy-nine men had been killed and another eight wounded. The horses lost gravely weakened Wood's mounted force. The Border Horse was finished as a unit and the battalions of Zulu irregulars had decamped. Fortunately, the warriors of the main impi had been so tired and short of food that, after decimating the men of Barton and Weatherley on the Ityentika Nek, they had halted to make camp; thus more of Buller's men had managed to escape than would otherwise have been the case. It was clear, however, that the impi would be coming on next day.

Although the action of the 28th could not be counted a success, Wood was reasonably confident that the impi would attack him at Kambula as he desired, and not bypass him to move directly on Utrecht. Soon after dawn on the 29th Raaf's Transvaal Rangers rode out to locate the impi. The cattle were put out to graze and, after some deliberation, Wood despatched two companies of the 13th to collect firewood for his field bakeries. Uys' burghers announced that they wished to trek home now that their leader was dead.

By 11 a.m. Raaf had returned to report that the impi was on the move; he brought with him one of Uhamu's men who had learned that the Zulus were going to attack at about noon. Wood also received information that the impi was some 24,000 strong, consisting of regiments which had defeated No. 3 Column, together with the abaQulusi from Hlobane. Tshingwayo was again in command, his warriors were full of confidence, and many had rifles taken from the 24th at Isandhlwana and the 80th at the Intombi. Shortly after Raaf's return the impi was spotted 5 miles away across the plain, coming on due westwards in five columns. The wood-cutting party came in, the cattle were driven into the kraal, and Wood, confident that the defences could be manned within a minute and a half from the 'Alarm' being sounded, ordered the men to have their dinners.

At about 12.45 the tents were struck, the reserve ammunition in opened boxes was distributed, and the troops took up their battle stations. One company each of the 1/13th and 90th was sited in the redoubt with two 7-pounders; another company of the 1/13th was in the cattle kraal; and the balance of the infantry manned the laager, with the 90th holding the north-west sides and the 1/13th the south-east. The other four 7-pounders took post in the open, facing north between the laager and the redoubt; the gunners were told that if the Zulus got in close they were to abandon the guns and shelter in the laager. In all, Wood's force mustered 121 Royal Artillery and Royal Engineers, 1,238 infantry, and 638 mounted men including the Mounted Infantry; with the headquarters staff it totalled 2,000, of which 88 men were sick in hospital. As the troops moved to their posts, they could see the two right-hand Zulu columns forming the right horn veer off to the north, circling round out of artillery range until they halted north-west of the camp. The other three forming their left and centre continued on westwards until they were due south of Kambula.

The ground to the north of the position ran off in a gentle downward slope, but on the other side the field of fire was limited to between 100 and 200 yards, beyond which a low cliff, forming the southern flank of the Kambula ridge, fell into a ravine where ran the headwaters of the White Umfolozi. Further to the west along the cliff-top, about 300 yards from the laager, was the garrison's refuse tip on which clumps of mealies and long grass had grown rapidly in the horse manure. The southward approaches, therefore, offered considerable cover to the Zulu left and centre.

At 1.30 Buller suggested he sting the right horn into a premature attack, to which Wood agreed. The mounted men rode out to within range of the massed Zulus, fired a volley, and then galloped back, followed closely by the Nokenke, umBonambi and umCijo in a great black wave of 11,000 warriors. The Edendale troop of Natal Native Horse, which had been at Isandhlwana and had no intention of getting caught in another pitched battle, made off to the west, but the Colonials rode hard for the laager, dismounting therein to thicken up the infantry's rifle fire with their carbines. As soon as the horsemen had cleared their front the 90th opened up with volleys, supported by the four 7-pounders firing shell until the Zulus were within 400 yards, when they changed to case-shot; the companies in the redoubt enfiladed the left flank of the enemy charge.

Although a small number of the Zulus managed to burst into the laager, where they were turned out with bayonets, the advance was generally held by the steady musketry and gunfire at between 200 and 400 yards. Some of the Zulus swung right to come in against the western sides of the laager but were no more successful here than on the north. After about half an hour's fighting the right horn drew back out of range to the north-east.

While they made off, the left horn and centre, inGobamakhosi, Undi and abaQulusi, came surging up out of the ravine at about 2.15. As they came over the crest they were met by a cross-fire from the southern face of the laager and the cattle kraal which blasted the leading warriors. More and more, however, swarmed on to the glacis between the cliff and the defenders, funnelling into the gap between the laager and kraal. Since the narrowest part of the glacis lay in front of the kraal, the Zulus in that area soon forced their way into it and fought hand-to-hand with the 1/13th company stationed there. Both sides were hampered by the cattle in the kraal, but with the Zulu pressure building up the heavily outnumbered soldiers managed to extricate themselves from the mêlée and pull back to the redoubt. This allowed Zulu riflemen to open fire from behind the walls of the kraal to cover the advance of their comrades further along the cliff-face.

At about the same time the right horn came on again from the north-east, charging across the north face of the redoubt towards the guns and the eastern sides of the laager. Though he was now attacked on both sides, Wood appreciated that the situation on the southern flank was more critical. He therefore ordered Major Hackett with two companies of the 90th to clear the Zulus off the glacis. Hackett doubled his men out of the laager, formed them in line with fixed bayonets, and charged across the open ground, driving the Zulus over the rim.

The 90th then lined the crest and opened volley fire into the packed warriors in the ravine. The counter-attack had succeeded perfectly, but then Hackett's men suddenly found themselves under fire from their right, where numbers of inGobamakhosi marksmen had concealed themselves among the refuse tip. Hackett had the 'Retire' sounded and his men regained the cover of the laager, but not before a colour-sergeant had been killed, one subaltern mortally wounded and Hackett himself had received a head wound which blinded him.

Men of C Company, 1/13th Light Infantry in Zululand.

The closing stages of the battle of Kambula. A company of the 1/13th in the foreground are driving the Zulus back into the ravine. To the left rear can be seen the main laager with beyond it the guns of 11/7 Battery in the open below the redoubt on the hillock, to the right of which is the cattle kraal. Water colour by Orlando Norie.

The sight of Hackett's withdrawal encouraged the Zulus in the ravine to charge again, but along the narrow killing zone in front of the laager their high courage and cowhide shields could not prevail against the 13th's controlled volleys from behind the wagons and the redoubt. On the north side the detachments of 11/7 R.A. fought their guns in the open, never taking cover, and pouring out round after round of shell and case into the right horn, covered by the rifles of the 90th. Both battalions fired only at the word of command, and so collected and well directed was their fire that at the end of the battle the expenditure of ammunition averaged only 33 rounds per man.

No matter how bravely the Zulus came on, as they did again and again, the head of each charge was shot away, and around 5 p.m. Wood sensed that the impetus was going out of their attack. He put two companies of the 13th in to clear the cattle kraal and lined the rim of the cliff with a third to open fire into the dead ground. As soon as he saw the Zulus in the ravine beginning to pull away eastwards, he ordered Buller to mount up and pursue.

It was a curious thing about the Zulus that, although they would attack with great courage and tenacity, once beaten and in retreat they would put up little resistance. Buller's men harried them mercilessly for 7 miles, shooting them one-handed with carbines from the saddle or spearing them with discarded assegais. The Frontier Light Horse singled out the abaQulusi for their special attention, chasing them as far as Hlobane and extracting a savage vengeance for their comrades who had died the day before.

Over 800 Zulu dead were counted in the immediate vicinity of the position and hundreds more perished in the ravine and during the pursuit. Eighteen British soldiers were killed, and eight officers and fifty-seven men wounded, of which eleven later died. Kambula was the turning point of the war, for it taught the Zulus the unhappy lesson that shield and assegai, no matter how courageously wielded, were no match for artillery and the Martini-Henry. Never again would an impi come on with the ferocity and resolution displayed up to this date. Four days later some of the regiments that had attacked at Kambula faced Chelmsford's square at Gingindhlovu. Whereas at Kambula the fighting had lasted four hours, at the latter it was all over in twenty minutes.

Cetshwayo had never wanted to fight, but he had been unable to restrain his unblooded warriors. By the time Kambula and Gingindhlovu had been fought, much blood had been spilled, his warriors were tired and dispirited, and he began to consider how the fighting could be ended. Chelmsford, on the other hand, with his strength greatly increased by the reinforcements from England, was determined to end it in his own way and vindicate his name.

PART III
THE SECOND INVASION

8
Preliminaries

By mid-April 1879, after Wood's convincing victory and with Eshowe relieved and evacuated, there were no British troops in Zululand except Wood's, who remained in the vicinity of Kambula and the garrison of the new Fort Chelmsford on the Inyezane. The reinforcements ordered out from home had all arrived and were camped at Durban, acclimatizing themselves to the South African sun after an English winter. The horses of the two regular cavalry regiments, the 1st King's Dragoon Guards and the 17th Lancers, were in poor shape after being cooped up on board ship, and took some time to recover their condition. Three more infantry battalions had landed, the 2/21st Royal Scots Fusiliers, the 58th and 94th, while the 1/24th had been reconstituted with a draft of 600 men, making fifteen battalions available in all. N/5 Battery had been reformed and, apart from 11/7 R.A. with Wood, the gunners in Natal now included M, N and O Batteries, 6th Brigade, Royal Field Artillery, and half the 10th Battery and one section of 8th Battery, 7th Brigade, Royal Garrison Artillery. 10/7 was equipped with four Gatlings and O/6 was employed as an ammunition column.

In addition to the Natal Horse, which had been formed, as mentioned earlier, from the Europeans of the disbanded 3rd N.N.C., there were other new colonial mounted units: the confusingly-named Natal Light Horse, about two troops strong, under an ex-officer of the 17th Lancers, Captain Whalley, who had served not only in the Sepoy Mutiny, China and Abyssinia but also in the Franco-Prussian and Carlist Wars; a corps of Mounted Rifles raised by the former commandant of the 3rd N.N.C., Rupert Lonsdale; and various small bodies of mounted Bantu scouts. Together with those already in the field, the mounted troops, other than the regular cavalry, now totalled some 1,400.

Among the reinforcements sent out from England were no fewer than four major-generals. In early February, dismayed by events and feeling at a low ebb, Chelmsford had written home asking for a second-in-command of major-general's rank, who could relieve him of some of his administrative problems, and be ready to assume command in the event of his health failing, a possibility of which he was then apprehensive. This letter was wrongly interpreted at home as a request to be replaced, which naturally proved harmful to Chelmsford's reputation, but it had not motivated the despatch of the four general officers, for these were already on the way when it was received in London. It was, however, to have other repercussions, as will be seen shortly. The senior of the four was Major-General Hon. Hugh Clifford, who had won the Victoria Cross with the Rifle Brigade in the Crimea. He had had considerable experience on the staff, but his abrasive manner made him a

Transports and warships lying off Durban.

difficult subordinate. The other three were H. H. Crealock (the brother of Chelmsford's military secretary), who had fought in the Crimea, the Mutiny, China and Canada, Edward Newdigate and Frederick Marshall.

The fights at Kambula and Gingindhlovu had demonstrated that the Zulu Army was no longer the menace it had been three months before. Any invasion of Natal was now most unlikely, but Chelmsford appreciated that, until Ulundi and Cetshwayo had been captured, the war could not be concluded. He further realized that the force he now had at his disposal was far larger than was necessary for this task, and its size would simply impose an even greater burden on his limited supply and transport resources. On the other hand, the additional generals and troops had arrived, so employment for them had to be found. He decided to form a striking force for Ulundi, which was to be supported on its right flank by a secondary column advancing up the coast from the Lower Tugela Drift. Because of the distance to Ulundi and the shortage of transport, it would not be possible for all the necessary stores to accompany the columns. Intermediate

Officers of the 17th Lancers off duty.

supply dumps would have to be set up along the lines of advance, at which the wagons would unload and then return to bring forward the rest of the stores. Thus the columns would have to be strong enough both to fight and to provide escorts for the wagons, as well as throwing off garrisons behind the advance.

Since he intended to command the main force in person, he placed the responsibility for all

Left: Horses of the King's Dragoon Guards on the banks of the Tugela.

Left, below: Major-General Frederick Marshall, in command of the cavalry of the Second Division, wearing an Afghan 'poshteen'. Water colour by Lt-Col. J. N. Crealock.

administrative arrangements within Natal and the security of the lines of communication up to the Zululand border under Clifford, giving him the equivalent of three regular battalions, some cavalry, and part of the N.N.C. for this purpose. The remaining troops were formed into two divisions: one for the coastal column under Crealock, the other under Newdigate to form the striking force together with Wood's command which was allowed to retain its separate identity as the newly-designated Flying Column.

The troops were allocated to duties as follows.

Natal and Lines of Communication. Major-General Clifford

Part of the Naval Brigade.
1st King's Dragoon Guards, less one squadron.
Elements, Colonial Mounted Volunteers.
2/4th Regiment.
2/24th Regiment.
Two companies, 2/21st Fusiliers.
One company, 1/24th Regiment.
Two companies, 58th Regiment.
Two companies, 94th Regiment.
Two battalions, Natal Native Contingent.

Coastal Column. First Division. Major-General Crealock

Naval Brigade, less detachments in Natal. (Three 9-pounders, four 24-pounder rockets, four Gatlings.)

121

Officers and men of 10/7 Battery, Royal Artillery, the first Gatling gun battery formed in the Army. Major J. F. Owen, commanding, stands by the near wheel of the left-hand gun.

Officers of the 2nd Battalion, 21st Royal Scots Fusiliers, at dinner in camp. Their glengarries have a diced band but otherwise they are dressed as English infantry, tartan trews not being adopted until after 1881.

Camp of Captain Bettington's troop, Natal Horse, at Stanger.

The reorganized Natal Native Contingent with the First Division. Most of the men now have uniforms and rifles.

Colonial Mounted Volunteers (564). (As at Gingindhlovu, plus Lonsdale's Mounted Rifles.)
John Dunn's Scouts.
Artillery:
    M/6 Battery, R.F.A. (six 7-pounders).
    One section, 8/7 Battery, R.G.A. (two 7-pounders).
    One section, 11/7 Battery, R.G.A. (two 7-pounders).
    Half O/6 Battery, R.F.A. (Ammunition column).
1st Brigade. Colonel Pearson, 3rd Buffs.
    2/3rd Regiment.
    88th Regiment.
    99th Regiment.

2nd Brigade. Colonel Clarke, 57th.
    57th Regiment.
    3/60th Rifles.
    91st Highlanders.

Ulundi Column. Lieutenant-General Lord Chelmsford
Second Division. Major-General Newdigate.
    Cavalry Brigade. Major-General Marshall.
        One squadron, 1st King's Dragoon Guards.
        17th Lancers.
        Natal Horse.
        One troop, Natal Native Horse.
    Artillery and Engineers.
        N/5 Battery, R.F.A. (six 7-pounders).

N/6 Battery, R.F.A. (six 9-pounders).
Half O/6 Battery, R.F.A. (Ammunition column).
5th Field Company, Royal Engineers.
1st Brigade. Colonel Collingwood, 21st.
   2/21st Fusiliers, less two companies.
   58th Regiment, less two companies.
2nd Brigade. Colonel Glyn, 24th.
   1/24th Regiment, less one company.
   94th Regiment, less two companies.
One battalion, Natal Native Contingent.

Flying Column. Brigadier-General Wood.
   Cavalry (784). Lieutenant-Colonel Buller.
      One squadron, Imperial Mounted Infantry.
      Colonial Mounted Volunteers. (As at Kambula, plus Natal Light Horse.)
   Artillery.
      11/7 Battery, R.G.A., less one section (four 7-pounders).
      Half 10/7 Battery, R.G.A. (four Gatlings).
   Infantry.
      1/13th Light Infantry.
      80th Regiment, less four companies.
      90th Light Infantry.
      One battalion, Natal Native Contingent.

The two best routes into Zululand, from Rorke's Drift and the Lower Tugela Drift, were about equidistant from Ulundi. Chelmsford's choice of the northerly route for the main advance was influenced by the facts that there would be fewer rivers to cross, that those which would be encountered presented less of an obstacle than those near the coast, and that there would be more fuel available for the field bakeries and ovens. Furthermore his most reliable and proven commander, Evelyn Wood, was already in the north. On the other hand, the assembly of the troops and supplies for such an advance would involve a much longer haul up from Durban than a concentration at the Lower Drift.

Therefore Crealock, who arrived at the Lower Drift to take command of the First Division on 18 April, found himself with a less than adequate wagon train to carry out his tasks. These were to establish an intermediate staging post on the Amatikulu and an advanced base beyond on the Inyezane containing supplies for two months. He was then to destroy the military kraals at emaNgwene and Undi, just south of the Umhlatuzi River, thereafter advancing across that river to the mission station of St Paul's, 25 miles from Ulundi. Each of his wagons would have to make at least three journeys between the Lower Drift and the advanced base before all the supplies could be moved forward, a round trip of some 40 miles over deteriorating tracks with diminished grazing for the cattle.

Chelmsford had made his appreciation of the situation and issued his orders by mid-April, but it was to be the end of May before the main column was ready to advance. Although he believed the route that was originally to have been taken by the ill-fated No. 3 Column to be the most suitable for his advance to Ulundi, he hesitated to march the newly-arrived battalions of the Second Division past Isandhlwana, where the corpses of 22 January still mouldered. Therefore it would be necessary to make a detour to avoid that place of unhappy memories before striking the route some way beyond it in the region of Isipezi Hill or Ibabanango. The border along the Buffalo could be crossed at the Middle Drift, but the country beyond was thought unsuitable for the passage of a column heading northwards to Ulundi. He would have to select an entry point north of Rorke's Drift, basing his advance not on Helpmakaar but on Dundee or even further north on Utrecht. An advance from Dundee would, however, have to cross both the Buffalo and Blood Rivers. Although a track running roughly eastwards from Dundee crossed the Buffalo at Landman's Drift, thereafter it led northwards for about 20 miles until it reached the nearest known drift across the Blood near Conference Hill, beyond which lay Kambula another 12 miles to the north-east. Wood's mounted patrols had found a track from Kambula

Lord Chelmsford seated between Col. Evelyn Wood, on his right, and Lt-Col. Redvers Buller with members of his staff: from left, Lt-Col. J. N. Crealock, Capt. Molyneux and Major Gosset.

Tents of the Second Division Camp.

The Gatling guns of 10/7 Battery, Royal Artillery. The Battery-Sergeant-Major in front of the right-hand gun wears a blue serge frock and booted overalls. His sword is suspended by slings from a brown leather waistbelt and his revolver is attached to a cross belt over the right shoulder; the subaltern on his right has a similar revolver belt. The bombardier at extreme right wears a tunic and carries his revolver on his waistbelt.

Infantry of the Second Division standing to at dawn in the camp at Landman's Drift. An Illustrated London News *engraving after a sketch by Melton Prior.*

The 17th Lancers in camp. Note the lances between the tents.

leading south-east towards Ibabanango but, as far as was known, the country on the Zulu side of the Blood eastwards from Landman's Drift was impassable. Thus it appeared that, to avoid using the Helpmakaar–Isandhlwana–Ibabanango route, a distance of about 45 miles, the main column would have to make a huge loop to the north, from Dundee via Landman's Drift and Conference Hill, before turning south towards Ibabanango; a detour about twice as long. Despite the extra time and strain on his transport resources such a detour would entail, Chelmsford's aversion to the Isandhlwana track was so strong that he determined on the longer route, nominating Conference Hill as the advanced supply base for the Second Division and the Flying Column, the latter still camped at Kambula. Once the decision had been made, the newly-arrived regiments entrained at Durban for Pietermaritzburg, thence marching north to Dundee, 120 miles away, and on to Landman's Drift, while the wagon convoys rolled north to stock the new base at Conference Hill.

By mid-May the regiments of the Second Division had reached their concentration area after a long march which had served to toughen them up and break them in to South African field conditions. According to a soldier of the 58th, which had left England in snow and slush at the end of February, the effects of the sea journey on the early stages of the march, with 'inaction, want of exercise and none-too-liberal supply of nourishing diet, coupled with our heavy loads, under a burning sun made sad work of us'. Not until they were encouraged, by more seasoned troops, to 'throw away them packs' were the men from peacetime garrisons at home able to make better progress. By the time they encamped at the end of their long march they felt less green beside the old stagers who had been in the field since January. Meanwhile the Flying Column had left Kambula and set up a new camp at Wolf Hill, 12 miles east of Conference Hill.

On 18 May a patrol of the 17th Lancers returned to Dundee to report that it had found a crossing place over the Blood River just south of Koppie Allein and less than 10 miles east of Landman's Drift; beyond it a track suitable for wagons ran east past Itelezi Hill, and then turned south towards Isipezi Hill and Ibabanango. It is difficult to understand how this had not been discovered before Chelmsford

127

A corporal of the 17th Lancers. His tunic is buttoned over on the left side to hide the white plastron. Water colour by Alphonse de Neuville.

selected Conference Hill as the advanced base. Be that as it may, the discovery meant that the Blood could be crossed some 20 miles further south. In the long run this would save wear and tear on the transport, not to mention time; but, to make use of it, all the supplies laboriously moved up to Conference Hill would now have to be fetched down again to be dumped in a new base at Koppie Allein.

The time it would take to put the revised arrangements into effect gave Chelmsford the opportunity to undertake a task he had long been under pressure from Natal to carry out — the burial of the four-month-old corpses at Isandhlwana. A small patrol had visited Fugitive's Drift on 4 February and had buried the bodies of Melvill and Coghill at the place where they had perished. Some way off

downstream the tattered Queen's Colour of the 1/24th, which the two men had died trying to save, was found in a pool. It was handed over amid scenes of some emotion to Colonel Glyn who received it on behalf of the re-formed battalion. When the 1/24th returned to England after the war, Queen Victoria placed a wreath of immortelles upon the Colour in permanent memorial of the officers and men who had died. In March another patrol had visited Isandhlwana, but without digging tools had been unable to bury the dead who all still lay where they had fallen. No trace was found of the 2/24th's Colours, although the pike of one was discovered much later in a Zulu kraal. Since then, no one had been to the site, as Chelmsford had been unwilling to risk sending a detachment so far into Zululand to perform

Lieutenant-Colonel W. P. Collingwood, 21st Royal Scots Fusiliers, commanding the 1st Brigade, Second Division. Note the gaiters worn by infantry officers which were longer than the men's and fastened with buttons instead of lacing.

of his regiment be left where they were until detachments of both battalions could be assembled to bury their comrades. So on the 21st only the dead of the Natal units were interred and it would be another month before the battlefield was finally cleared. All the remains were placed in shallow graves surmounted by cairns of stones, which can be seen to this day, dotting the plain in front of Isandhlwana.

As the end of May approached the preparations for the advance of the Second Division and Flying Column were nearly complete. To the south Crealock's 2nd Brigade was at Fort Chelmsford on the Inyezane but his 1st had not yet left the Lower Drift, while his wagons were still shuttling back and forth between the two. It was to take until 19 June before the whole of the First Division was concentrated with its supplies at Fort Chelmsford, ready to advance. Eight weeks had passed since Kambula and Gingindhlovu, but Chelmsford had been determined to leave

what might prove to be a lengthy and unpleasant task which, no matter how offended the sensibilities of the Natal clergy and settlers might be by its neglect, stood low in the scale of military priorities. Now that he had a sufficiency of mounted troops and the necessary route reconnaissances for the second invasion had been completed, he felt able to attend to it.

Major-General Marshall rode down with some cavalry to Rorke's Drift where he collected five companies of the 2/24th and a large party of Natal Volunteers. They reached Isandhlwana on 21 May and, after posting the infantry as protective picquets on the high ground, set about searching for the bodies, by now mostly skeletons, concealed in the long grass. Colonel Glyn had requested that the dead

Mr McKenzie, war correspondent of the Standard.

129

A romanticized version by Alphonse de Neuville of the finding of the bodies of Lieutenants Melvill and Coghill. The uniforms are accurately depicted but the 17th Lancers were not present when the bodies were found and the Queen's Colour of the 1/24th, not the Regimental as shown, was discovered some way off.

Two officers of the 4th Natal Native Contingent, First Division.

Transport staff officers of the Flying Column.

A corporal and privates of the 58th Regiment working a heliograph with the Second Division.

A field butchery of the Second Division.

nothing to chance for his second trial with the enemy. The administrative arrangements had without doubt been the cause of much of the delay, but in any case there was no great urgency about launching his final offensive since the Zulus would not disappear and there was no chance of his accepting any terms that might be offered by Cetshwayo. Had Chelmsford been aware, during those eight weeks, of deliberations taking place in London, he might have impelled his subordinates to speedier action.

When the news of the disastrous start to the war had reached London on 11 February, the first reaction of the Cabinet had been to pull Chelmsford's chestnuts out of the fire by authorizing sufficient reinforcements to ensure that he could not fail twice. Its next step was to take some of the heat out of the Opposition's attacks on its policies and to assuage public opinion by laying the blame on the perpetrator of the war – Sir Bartle Frere. Though Disraeli was furious with Frere for his high-handed action in presenting Cetshwayo with the ultimatum, he had stopped short of recalling him, but had delivered a sharp reprimand for acting without Government approval. Because the rebuke was given wide publicity, the Government might just as well have removed Frere from his post, as his authority was now thoroughly undermined. As far as Chelmsford was concerned, the defeat at Isandhlwana and his request for a second-in-command had shaken Disraeli's confidence in him, but it was not politic to replace him before he had had the chance to redeem himself, once the reinforcements had arrived. In any case Disraeli knew that Chelmsford had the backing of the Queen and the Duke of Cambridge, who would have resisted any attempt to remove him. Once the news of Kambula and Gingindhlovu was received, it seemed that the decision to

Officers of the 88th Connaught Rangers with the First Division.

133

leave him in command had been justified. Nevertheless doubts about his capacity still remained.

The over-all picture of affairs in South Africa gave the Government little cause for satisfaction. The Zulus still had to be overcome, Chelmsford remained at odds with Sir Henry Bulwer over Natal's contribution to the war, and events in the Transvaal boded ill for the future. Shepstone's ineffective administration had led to his departure, officially on leave, in January, leaving affairs in the hands of the comparatively junior Colonel Owen Lanyon, and the increasingly militant Boers had only just been dissuaded from armed rebellion in March by some swift talking from Frere, fortunately just before his censure from the Cabinet became public knowledge. It seemed to the Government that the direction of affairs in South Africa was too fragmented, and that what was needed was someone who could assume over-all control of civil and military affairs in Natal, the Transvaal and Zululand. The only man with a sufficiently high military reputation and experience of civil administration, as well as familiarity with the problems of South Africa, was Sir Garnet Wolseley, then the overlord of Cyprus, which had been acquired by Britain from Turkey in 1878 as a convenient base in the eastern Mediterranean.

Wolseley, then aged forty-six, had seen service as a regimental and staff officer in Burma, the Crimea and the Mutiny. He had made his reputation as Britain's 'only general' by his bloodless campaign against some Canadian half-breeds in the Red River Expedition of 1870 and his well-planned conquest of the Ashantis in West Africa three years later; both had required more skill as an organizer and administrator than strategic or tactical brilliance. His enthusiasm for all manner of military reform, including Cardwell's short-service system which during a short spell at the War Office between his two campaigns he had done much to advance, had made him 'the very model of a modern major-general' and

therefore the sworn enemy of that bastion of military reaction, the Duke of Cambridge, thus earning for himself neither the liking nor the admiration of the Queen. He was undoubtedly much cleverer than the majority of his peers and his urgings for military reform were almost wholly justified, but his snobbery, ambition, conceit and favouritism towards his 'Ring' – a circle of Wolseley-approved officers – all conspired to earn him the dislike and distrust of the more conservative and self-effacing elements in the Army. Among politicians, whom he despised, and the general public, his stock stood high. His speedy despatch of the Ashantis, in which he had been responsible for both military and civil affairs, had earned him the approbation of Lord Carnarvon, then Colonial Secretary, who had asked for the loan of his services in 1874 so that he might be appointed Lieutenant-Governor of Natal, with the specific task of persuading the colony of the merits of confederation, for which it would have to surrender the autonomy it had enjoyed hitherto. By dint of some rather sharp, hustling tactics he succeeded, and in August 1875 he had handed over his post to Bulwer.

After three years in London he received the Cyprus appointment, but his self-esteem at being chosen for the job was soon deflated by the realization that no fame awaited him therein. Despite his prestige he was well aware that no undertaking really worthy of his talents had yet come his way. He hungered for a European war or, failing that, a major colonial campaign. He was kicking his heels in increasing frustration with Cyprus when the Afghan War broke out. He immediately signified his readiness to leave for India at once, but to his chagrin he was told that there was a sufficiency of general officers on the spot.

When he heard the news of Isandhlwana he became certain that the Government could no longer deny him the opportunity he craved, and to clinch matters telegraphed to Whitehall requesting that he be sent to the Cape. To his relief the summons came. Not even an

Commandant Raaf and officers of the Transvaal Rangers.

Captain James, R.E., of the Intelligence Department of Chelmsford's headquarters.

2nd Battalion, 21st Royal Scots Fusiliers, at church parade in the field before the second invasion. The officer behind the padre is Lt-Col. Collingwood and the bearded soldier in tartan trews six from the left is probably a piper.

unpleasant interview with the Duke of Cambridge, in which the latter ascribed Chelmsford's defeat entirely to the short-service system, could spoil Wolseley's satisfaction at being appointed 'Governor of Natal and the Transvaal and High Commissioner for native and foreign affairs to the north and east of those colonies' (i.e. Zululand), with the local rank of full general. With this commission in his pocket he was endowed with complete military and civilian powers over Frere, Bulwer, Chelmsford and Lanyon in all those territories; only Frere's governorship of Cape Colony remained outside his jurisdiction.

Although the chance of emerging as the conqueror of Zululand and the overseer of southern Africa's future had come later than he would have wished, he believed there was still time for him to reach the Cape, take over the operations against the Zulus and bring them to a triumphant conclusion, thus greatly enhancing his fame and later career. Two days after his appointment was announced on 26 May, and nearly three weeks before the first news of their supersession reached Frere and Chelmsford, Wolseley sailed for the Cape accompanied by a select band of staff officers from his famous 'Ring'. His appointment found

little favour with the Queen and Cambridge, but his departure took place amid cheering crowds.

Three days later, on 31 May, the leading brigade of the Second Division, the 2/21st and 58th, supported by N/5 Battery, crossed the Blood River below Koppie Allein and set up camp on the far bank. The 2nd Brigade was to cross on the following day while the 1st Brigade advanced to the next camp at Itelezi Hill, and the Flying Column moved down from their starting point 18 miles to the north-east. The two columns were due to link up in the valley between the Ityotosi and Tombokola Rivers on 2 June. Newdigate had supplies for two months and Wood for six weeks but there was insufficient transport to move them all in one lift. Intermediate supply dumps would have to be established along the line of march and the empty wagons sent back to Koppie Allein to bring forward the balance, a process which would inevitably slow up the rate of advance. Inconvenient though this was, Chelmsford was not unduly perturbed by it at this stage, for as yet he knew nothing of the coming of Wolseley. Indeed he was quite composed. He had a strong, well-founded force of all arms, his subordinates were sound, the troops were in good shape, and he had little doubt that once the Zulus were encountered they could be overcome in short order. The setbacks and disappointments of the previous five months at last seemed to be behind him. Little did he know that within only two days of entering Zululand he was to be dealt yet another shattering blow.

General Sir Garnet Wolseley.

9

Misbehaviour before the Enemy

Staff officers seldom feature in accounts of military operations, which tend to concentrate on the commanders who plan and lead the operations and the units and formations that carry them out. Nevertheless the staff perform a vital function as a link between the commander and his troops, for it is they who translate the commander's plan into orders and make the necessary arrangements for the implementation of those orders. Although the nature of their work imposes a heavy burden and responsibility upon staff officers, they are less likely to be exposed to the dangers faced by regimental officers. Yet it was during the performance of a simple staff duty that the next calamity of the Zulu War was to occur; a calamity that was to have an even more shattering impact than Isandhlwana.

Chelmsford's Assistant-Quartermaster-General was Lieutenant-Colonel Richard Harrison, Royal Engineers, whose responsibilities for the second invasion of Zululand included the reconnaissance of routes and the selection of camp sites for the column's advance. Since Zululand had not been properly surveyed, this task required the preparation of rudimentary maps based on sketches made by staff officers of the terrain ahead of the advance. To assist him in his duties, Harrison was allocated one of a number of unattached officers who had been sent out with the reinforcements, a certain Lieutenant Carey of the 98th Regiment, who was appointed Deputy-Assistant-Quartermaster-General.

Carey, then in his 32nd year, was the son of a clergyman who had christened him with the unusual name of Jaheel, a figure from the Old Testament whose tribe 'were a people that jeoparded their lives unto death in the high places of the field'. Compared with many officers of his age and seniority Carey was somewhat singular. He had been educated not at a public school, as most of his contemporaries had been, but in France where he acquired certain Gallic characteristics which ensured him a measure of intimidation from his more conventional fellows at the Royal Military College, Sandhurst, which he entered in 1864. His financial circumstances only allowed him to take a commission in the socially inferior and inexpensive 3rd West India Regiment, with whom he served during some minor punitive expeditions in West Africa and British Honduras. The disbandment of that regiment in 1870 forced him to go on half-pay and he returned to France to join an English ambulance unit assisting in the Franco-Prussian War. In 1871 he was restored to full pay with a lieutenancy in the 81st Regiment, exchanging into the 98th a year later. Being an ambitious man, and with a wife and family to support, he applied to enter the Staff College at Camberley, an institution to which in those days few regimental officers aspired; those who did frequently incurred the displeasure of their commanding officers and their regiments, unless it was felt that they would not be missed. Having passed the entrance examination, Carey arrived at the College in 1877, from which he emerged after nearly two years' grinding study just as the Zulu War broke out. On hearing the news of Isandhlwana he immediately volunteered for South Africa to serve in any capacity. He joined Harrison's staff in early May and the skills he had acquired at the Staff College in map-making and reconnaissance soon earned him a reputation as 'an officer of outstanding promise and a glutton for duty'.

Notwithstanding Carey's ability and zeal, Harrison was still short-handed, for the second invasion involved constant labour and worry. It was with mixed feelings, however, that he received in mid-May another assistant, a young man who, though he wore the uniform of the Royal Artillery, was neither a regular, a colonial nor even an ordinary civilian. He was, in fact, the only son of the late Emperor Napoleon III and the Empress Eugénie: Louis, Prince Imperial of France.

Born in 1856, Louis had been brought up since childhood to a belief in and a desire for military glory, his days spent among the glittering spectacle of an army with which his father hoped to re-create the great epoch of the First Empire. As a boy of fourteen Louis had accompanied the Emperor to the front in the opening weeks of the Franco-Prussian War, only to see the army which he had been taught was invincible exposed as a sham. In less than two months from the outbreak of war, with his father captured at Sedan, Louis and his mother had been forced to seek sanctuary in England, where the following year they were joined in exile by the ex-Emperor, who died two years later.

Queen Victoria had initially found the presence of the Bonapartes politically embarrassing but she took pity on their plight. After Napoleon had asked for something to be done for his son, it had been agreed that Louis should enter the Royal Military Academy, Woolwich, where potential officers of the Royal Artillery and Royal Engineers were trained. Louis soon made himself popular with his fellow cadets, entered into the work with enthusiasm, impressed everyone with his horsemanship, and in 1875 passed out seventh in his class of thirty-four. He could not be granted a commission in the Royal Artillery as he would have wished, but was allowed to serve with a battery at Aldershot during manoeuvres. As far as France was concerned there was little likelihood of a Bonaparte restoration, but Frenchmen of that persuasion regarded him as Napoleon IV, whereas Republicans viewed his career and public persona with emotions that varied from contempt to grudging respect.

When the reinforcements began to sail for South Africa in February 1879, Louis begged to be allowed to go with them so as to prove himself on active service. Disraeli, wary of French reactions, refused to entertain the notion at first, but, when confronted by a coalition of the Queen, Eugénie and the Duke of Cambridge, who combined to plead Louis' cause, he yielded on condition that Louis went out in a private capacity as a spectator. Triumphant, Louis sailed on 28 February bearing a letter from Cambridge to Chelmsford, in which the latter was asked to assist the Prince 'to see as much as he can with the columns in the field'. He also bore a letter of recommendation as to his military qualities from the Governor of Woolwich; both letters uttered words of warning about Louis' impulsiveness.

Chelmsford was scarcely overjoyed at the prospect of adding to his responsibilities the safety of a claimant to the throne of a country hardly well disposed to Britain, and in which voices had already been raised in protest at the lèse-majesté of sending a Bonaparte to serve in a junior appointment in the British Army. Nevertheless Chelmsford resignedly took Louis on his staff as an extra A.D.C. insisting, as

Lieutenant J. B. Carey, 98th Regiment, D.A.Q.M.G., at Chelmsford's headquarters.

Louis himself wished, that he be treated exactly as any other officer. Within days, however, Chelmsford's misgivings were realized when Louis' hotheadedness while accompanying a patrol led by Buller resulted in the latter's refusal to accept responsibility for him again.

Chelmsford attached him to Harrison to lend a hand with the survey work, giving orders that Louis was never to leave camp unless accompanied by an officer and an escort. Louis quickly made friends with the French-speaking Carey, who was flattered by the Prince's company and charmed by his enthusiasm.

Carey was now busy under Harrison's direction mapping the route for the imminent advance of the Second Division. Harrison wanted to make a last reconnaissance, and set out with Carey and an escort commanded by Commandant Bettington of the Natal Horse.

He had not wished to take the Prince along, but after Louis had obtained Chelmsford's permission he could not refuse. During the second day out the patrol came under a scattered fire from a party of Zulus hidden among some rocks. Drawing his great-uncle's sword, which he always carried, Louis charged excitedly behind Bettington to disperse the Zulus, who quickly fled. He returned to camp elated at being under fire, but when Chelmsford heard of the incident he wrote in a letter to his wife: 'The Prince Imperial nearly came to grief. I shall not let him out of my sight again if I can help it.'

There is no doubt that although everyone with whom Louis came into contact was captivated by his charm and eagerness, his presence was an embarrassment to Chelmsford and his staff. Despite Chelmsford's insistence

Louis Napoleon, Prince Imperial of France, as a gentleman cadet of the Royal Military Academy, Woolwich.

The Prince Imperial in 1879.

The Prince Imperial's horse, Percy. The groom is a Royal Artilleryman, in full dress tunic.

Funeral parade for the Prince Imperial at the Second Division camp. Chelmsford and staff stand behind the gun carriage bearing the Prince's body. The 17th Lancers parade dismounted with lances reversed beyond.

Troops lining the route for the Prince Imperial's funeral procession at Pietermaritzburg.

Board erected by the Royal Scots Fusiliers to mark the spot where the Prince Imperial fell.

that he was to be given no special treatment, his status as a royal prince made it difficult for them to curb his impetuosity and his keenness not to miss anything. On the other hand, they were all busy men with more important things on their minds than the need for constant supervision of a lively young man with no official position in the force. So it was that, when Louis approached Harrison with a request on the evening of 31 May, the day the invasion began, the latter's consideration of it was not as careful as it should have been. Louis asked if, on the next day, he could extend the sketches he had been making of the terrain beyond the next campsite at Itelezi Hill to the area the column was due to reach on 2 June between the Ityotosi and Tombokola Rivers. The ground in question had already been reported clear of Zulus and in any case there would be mounted patrols out guarding the advance of the main column to Itelezi. Harrison agreed on condition that Louis was accompanied by a proper escort of at least six colonials and six of the Edendale troop. He did not specify an officer to command the escort, as he assumed that Bettington would do so as on the previous patrol. When Carey heard of Louis' intentions he asked leave to accompany him to which Harrison, though he could ill spare him, gave his assent, so that Carey could keep an eye on the Prince.

Bettington personally selected six reliable men from his troop as the escort: Sergeant Willis, Corporal Grubb, Troopers Abel, Cochrane, Rogers and Le Tocq, a French-speaking Channel Islander, together with a Zulu guide. Bettington was unable to go himself, as he had already been detailed for another task, but knowing Carey was going he assumed he would be in command. On the following morning, Sunday 1 June, the men reported as ordered, but there was no sign of the men from the Edendale troop; they had in fact been detailed but in the confusion of the camp packing up they had reported to the wrong tent. On inquiring for them Carey was told to take six others from the advanced patrols they would pass through as they rode east and, since Louis was impatient to be off, they set out.

They soon overtook Harrison who was riding ahead to inspect the camp site at Itelezi. He noted Bettington's absence but, since Carey was with the patrol, did not comment on it, though he did ask where the Edendale men were. Carey explained and then, seeing that Louis had ridden on, called out to him to wait. Harrison told him to carry on and not to interfere with the Prince; an admonition which Harrison probably intended as no more than a warning not to nag the Prince or interfere with the sketching task he had given him, but which Carey was to interpret quite differently. Meanwhile Chelmsford, preparing to leave the Blood River camp, had asked where Louis was and had been told by a staff officer that he had ridden out with Harrison. Satisfied, the General turned his mind to the Division's advance to Itelezi.

As Louis and Carey rode eastwards they saw the advanced patrol disappearing from sight and Carey suggested they gallop after them to collect the other men for the escort. Louis demurred, saying that the six troopers they had with them were enough and Carey, who on a previous occasion had been mocked for taking an escort of eighty men on a reconnaissance, acquiesced. As the senior officer, Carey should have insisted that Harrison's order was obeyed, but he found it difficult to overrule Louis' natural air of authority. In any case, they were well mounted, had a good all-round view of the surrounding countryside and he had been told not to interfere; he therefore allowed command of the patrol to pass to the Prince.

Having arrived at the limit of their reconnaissance, Carey and Louis halted on some high ground to make their sketches. Some way off Louis spotted a deserted kraal on the north bank of the Ityotosi and suggested that they ride down to it so that they could collect water from the river and fuel from the huts to enable the men to make coffee. Noting that the huts were closely surrounded on three sides by tall clumps of mealies, Carey objected at first, but again allowed Louis to have his way. They reached the spot and knee-haltered the horses to allow them to graze. The mealies grew thick between the river and on either side of the huts; only on the north side was the ground open for a stretch of 200 yards until it fell into a dry donga some 8 feet deep. The troopers found signs of recent occupation and three dogs had slunk away at their approach, but as no other sign of life had been seen as they had ridden down Louis allowed the men to get on with brewing their coffee. He and Carey were soon deep in conversation, neither of them thinking to post a sentry; nor did the N.C.O.s consider it their place to remind them.

At about 3.30 Carey suggested it was time to move on, but Louis insisted there was no hurry. Suddenly the native guide ran in to say he had seen a Zulu over the hill. Louis told the men to collect their horses, which having scattered took ten minutes to effect, but at last the men were lined up at their horses' heads. Carey was already mounted and Louis gave the order: 'Prepare to mount.' Before he could complete the command, a volley of rifle shots crashed out and some thirty Zulus burst from the surrounding cover straight at the surprised patrol. Terrified by the sudden noise, the horses were difficult to control and Rogers' mount bolted, leaving him stranded. He managed to get off one shot before he was stabbed by an assegai. Carey, already in the saddle, was first away, riding hard for the donga, followed by Willis, Grubb and Cochrane, but Abel was shot in the back. Le Tocq dropped his carbine, dismounted to pick it up and somehow managed to clamber back on to his frightened animal. As he rode off he saw Louis running beside his horse, trying to vault into the saddle, and shouted at him in French to hurry. Louis' foot had slipped from the stirrup as his horse, a lively grey named Percy, reared up, but he managed to keep a grip on the holster attached to the front of the saddle. Running frantically beside the speeding animal he tightened his grip to swing up on to its back. As he did so, the leather of the holster ripped and he fell sprawling on the ground, the hooves smashing his right hand as the horse galloped away. He got up to see seven Zulus advancing on him with raised assegais. He reached for his sword but, finding it had fallen out, drew his revolver with his left hand and ran to a mound where he stood at bay. One of the Zulus threw an assegai which struck him in the thigh. He pulled it out and rushed at his assailant with it in his injured right hand, firing his revolver twice with his left. His shots missed. A second assegai stopped him in his tracks and the Zulus closed in, all of them stabbing until he was dead.

Carey pulled up on the far side of the donga where he was joined by Willis, Grubb, Cochrane and Le Tocq. He was appalled to see Louis' riderless grey gallop up, and when Le Tocq told him what he had seen, and as minutes passed without sign of the Prince, it seemed certain that he had been killed. If they went back to search for him, there appeared no hope of any of them escaping alive. Since the Zulus could be seen circling to cut them off, there was nothing for it but to ride for safety.

As the implications of the fearful incident, particularly for himself, sunk in, Carey's shock and horror were worsened when he approached Itelezi, since the first men to whom he had to break the dreadful news happened to be two of the bravest in the Army: Evelyn Wood and Redvers Buller. The latter told him bluntly he should be shot. As the story spread rapidly through the camp that night, Carey quickly realized that others held similar views and that he was to be cast in the role of scapegoat.

The Prince's death was a terrible blow to Chelmsford, coming as it did right at the start of the operations which were to wipe out the stain of the earlier disasters. All he could do was arrange for the recovery of the body, which was found to have seventeen stab wounds in it, all in front, and its removal to Durban for onward transmission to England, accompanied by suitable ceremonies which grew in scope and solemnity at every stage of its sad journey. Long before its arrival the news reached Europe by telegraph where it caused widespread horror in England and Anglophobic fury in France, even among Republicans who had mocked Louis' pretensions to the throne. Queen Victoria was distraught and the shock to the poor Empress left her semi-conscious for two days and inconsolable for weeks. The publicity this one death was given far outreached that accorded to the 1,300 casualties at Isandhlwana and many people must have wondered what further misfortunes the ill-fated and ill-conceived Zulu War still held in store. One thing at least was certain. As one heartless but pragmatic observer commented, the Zulus had inadvertently 'solved one of the most difficult problems of French history'.

Back in Zululand Carey's position became so invidious that he asked for a Court of Inquiry. This recommended that he be tried by General Court Martial on a charge of misbehaviour before the enemy when in command of an escort to the Prince Imperial in that, when attacked, he 'galloped away, not having attempted to rally the escort or in other ways defend the Prince'. In the eleven days that elapsed between the Prince's death and the trial, Carey's mood changed from grief to truculence, and he convinced himself that he had been illused. At his trial he defended himself coolly and without contrition, denying that he had been put in command of the escort, and claiming that its small numbers, the choice of resting place and the failure to post sentries were all due to Louis' assumption of the command. He insisted that when the Zulus made their surprise attack evasive action was the only course open, that he had rallied the survivors, and that since the Prince had clearly been killed, there was no point in hazarding the rest of the men's lives. The Court rejected his arguments, however, and, perhaps mindful of the similar charge pending against Harward for the Intombi affair, found him guilty. He was sentenced to be cashiered but with a recommendation for mercy. Neither findings nor sentence were to be revealed until they were confirmed by the authorities at home.

Carey returned to England expecting to be treated like a pariah, but found instead a wave of public sympathy for him generated by the Press who, without yet knowing the verdict of the Court, were apportioning much wider blame for the incident on Harrison, Chelmsford and even on the Duke of Cambridge. Carey embraced the role of martyr with enthusiasm, always ready to justify his actions, but his deliverance came ironically from Eugénie herself. Though well aware that Carey had abandoned her son, she wished for no re-criminations and no scapegoats, and con-sequently asked Victoria to intervene. The Queen did so and the proceedings of the Court were quashed 'on the grounds that the charge was not sustained by the evidence'. The public announcement completely exonerated Chelmsford, chided Harrison for unclear orders, and said that, although Carey had conceived a totally unjustified view of his relationship towards the Prince and had shown bad judgement, he was released from arrest and was to return to his regiment.

Stupidly, Carey did not let the matter rest and began to pester Eugénie for an audience, with the aim of finally vindicating himself. Eugénie ignored all his requests until, driven beyond endurance by his persistence, she sent his letters, which had grown increasingly contradictory and hypocritical, to the Queen. Appalled by what these letters disclosed of Carey's character, the Queen showed one of them to Disraeli, commenting that it was disgraceful that Carey had got off so lightly. Nevertheless the matter was allowed to rest.

Carey rejoined the 98th, but the immense and lengthy controversy his case had aroused, some papers condemning and others defending him, cannot have made the rest of his career easy, and the memory of those few moments on a hot Sunday afternoon in Zululand can never have been far from his mind, or the minds of those who came into contact with him. Perhaps the most charitable assessment of him was by a brother-officer of the 98th, who recalled that he was 'a very smart officer who had the bad luck not to have risen to the occasion when the opportunity arose'.

As things turned out, he did not have to endure the memory of that ill-fated afternoon for long as within four years he too was dead, succumbing to peritonitis at Karachi on 22 February 1883.

10

Ulundi

Notwithstanding the pall of gloom which the death of the Prince Imperial had cast over the camps of the Second Division and the Flying Column, the advance into Zululand had to go on and the force was put in motion on 3 June, the day after the Prince's body had left the camp. By the evening of the following day the Flying Column in the lead, having turned south-east at the Ityotosi, had reached the Nondweni River, while the Second Division bivouacked in Wood's vacated camp of the previous night.

Meanwhile Cetshwayo, who had been endeavouring to find ways of bringing the war to an end, had despatched envoys from Ulundi. These came before Chelmsford on 4 June and, although the burden of their message from the King was none too clear, Chelmsford understood that Cetshwayo wished to know what terms would be acceptable for a cessation of hostilities. After discussion, the General confined them to the handing over of all oxen which had been taken at Isandhlwana; the return of the two guns captured at the same battle; and the surrender of one entire regiment. To ensure that there could be no mis-understanding, the terms were put in writing and sent with the envoys to a Zulu-speaking Dutch trader, Cornelius Vijn, then living near Ulundi, who was to translate them to Cetshwayo.

On 5 June Buller took out the Frontier Light Horse to scout the way ahead, followed by General Marshall with a squadron each of the King's Dragoon Guards and the 17th Lancers. Zulus had been reported in the vicinity, and sure enough Buller's men encountered them on the far side of a stream. A brisk fire-fight developed, but when the enemy started to get round his flank Buller decided it was time to withdraw. The regular cavalry, however, eager for their first brush with the enemy, crossed the stream and, while the K.D.G.s guarded the flanks, Colonel Drury-Lowe of the 17th led his squadron in a series of charges. These achieved nothing, since the Zulus pulled back on to high ground where they opened fire on the lancers, in the course of which Lowe's adjutant, Lieutenant Frith, was killed. Somewhat chastened, the mounted force retired back to the east bank of the Nondweni where both the Flying Column and the Second Division were now concentrated.

Since the column had advanced some 30 miles from its supply bases, Chelmsford decided it was time to establish his first intermediate depot. On the 6th he began the construction of a fortified post, naming it Fort Newdigate, for which two companies of the 2/21st with two Gatlings of 10/7 Battery were told off as garrison. All the 660 wagons of both formations were off-loaded and sent back to Koppie Allein, escorted by the entire Flying Column. While they were away, Chelmsford started work on his next post, Fort Marshall,

147

Men of the 17th Lancers off duty. Note the variety of headdress, helmets, forage caps and cap comforters. Two of the seated men hold their Martini-Henry carbines.

nine miles south at Isipezi Hill on the main track to Ulundi, for which two more companies of the 21st were allocated.

It took Wood ten days to get the convoy back to the bases, reload the wagons and return to Fort Newdigate. By the time the force was once again complete and ready to advance, Chelmsford had received the first warning that Wolseley was on his way out to supersede him. With Ulundi only 50 miles away and with a month's supplies now in hand, Chelmsford had no intention of allowing Wolseley to reap the benefit of his preparations. The day after Wood's return, the 18th, he drove his column forward through Fort Marshall and on past Ibabanango where another post, Fort Evelyn, was constructed and two companies of the 58th left as garrison. With his unwieldy and slow-moving wagon train, however, he was only able to average about 4 miles a day, impeded by the single track and the drifts that crossed it.

On the day after Chelmsford left Fort Newdigate, Crealock was at last ready to begin his advance from the Inyezane with the First Division. Hampered by his shortage of wagons and with his oxen already flagging after shuttling the supplies up from the Lower Drift, it was not until the 22nd that his division was concentrated on the far side of the next river, the Umlalazi, only 6 miles further on. While an entrenched post, Fort Napoleon, was being constructed there, Crealock set out to find a stretch of beach where stores could be landed so as to avoid the long haul up by road. There were no natural harbours on this coastline, and the heavy surf made any landing difficult, if not impossible, but a calmer stretch was found 5 miles north of the mouth of the Umlalazi. This was called Port Durnford, and by the end of the month Crealock's Naval Brigade had rigged up a system of hawsers whereby supplies could be winched in from ships lying off shore.

On 23 June, five days after Chelmsford resumed his advance, Wolseley landed at Cape Town. He conferred briefly with Frere and sailed the next day for Durban, calling in at Port Elizabeth to fire off telegrams to Clifford, Crealock and Chelmsford, demanding immediate situation reports and insisting that all plans were to be referred to him. Reaching Durban on the 28th, he at once took the train to Pietermaritzburg, where he found replies from Clifford and Crealock but nothing from Chelmsford. Wolseley by now was in a fever of impatience. Although he had arrived too late to take over the final offensive against the Zulus at its outset, he was still determined that the credit for their overthrow should be his. His dilemma was to decide which of the two columns now advancing into Zululand he should best join to achieve this. He knew Crealock's location and clearly this was the easiest to reach, but the First Division's slow progress so far did not fill him with much confidence. On the other hand, Chelmsford's whereabouts were a mystery and telegraphic communication with him ended at Landman's Drift; beyond that all messages had to go by galloper. Because of this, Chelmsford had not received Wolseley's Port Elizabeth signal until late on the 28th, by which time he was 100 miles from Landman's Drift. Wolseley of course had no way of knowing this, and after another day had passed with still no word he sent off a furious signal on the 30th:

A fort garrisoned by men of the 2/21st.

149

A group of Royal Engineer officers with Chard wearing his Victoria Cross. He and the man on his left wear scarlet frocks, the others blue patrol jackets.

Part of the Flying Column: men of D Company, 1/13th Light Infantry with, at extreme left, the battalion Pioneer Sergeant (standing) and Quartermaster-Sergeant (kneeling). The men with bandoliers are mounted infantry and there are two bandsmen to the right of the front rank. The ammunition pouches of this battalion are of black, not buff, leather.

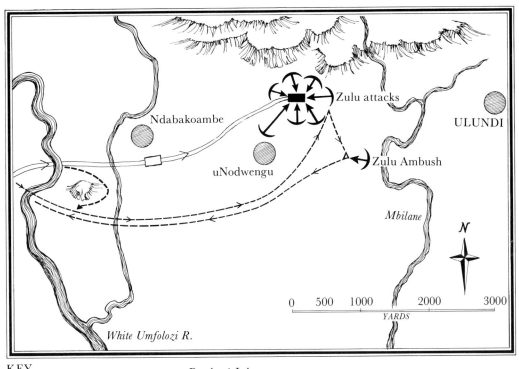

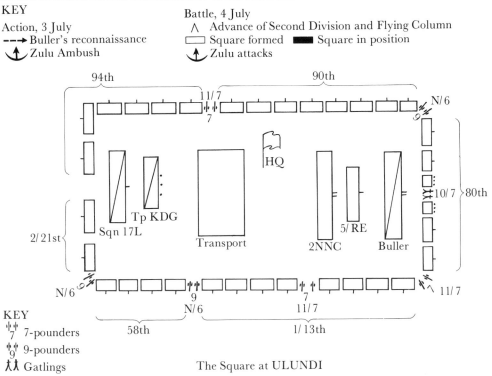

The Square at ULUNDI

Operations at Ulundi and Chelmsford's square

The staff of the Flying Column. Evelyn Wood (centre seated) is talking to Clery. Lysons is on the ground with Lord William Beresford immediately behind him.

'Concentrate your force immediately and keep it concentrated. Undertake no serious operations with detached bodies of troops. Acknowledge receipt of this message at once and flash back your latest moves. I am astonished at not hearing from you.' Later that day he learned that Crealock had established off-shore communications at Port Durnford. He decided that his only chance now lay in joining the First Division there and driving it on to Ulundi in the hope that he could snatch the victory he so hungered for, before Chelmsford could emerge from central Zululand. On the next day he returned to Durban. Before embarking for Port Durnford he sent off another signal to Chelmsford, saying that he was joining Crealock, and that Chelmsford was to fall back on the First Division should he be compelled to retreat. It was Wolseley, however, who had to retreat, for when he arrived off Port Durnford on 2 July the surf was too high for him to get ashore. After a miserable day with his frustration aggravated by sea-sickness, he was compelled to return to Durban to make arrangements to join Crealock by road on the 4th.

All his frantic efforts to reach the front had been in vain, for at the very time when he was riding north from Durban Chelmsford was about to engage the enemy. On 28 June, the day Wolseley's first telegram from Port Elizabeth was received, Chelmsford had reached Mtonjaneni, only 16 miles from Ulundi. There, he had again received Cetshwayo's envoys. They had conveyed his terms to the King through the offices of Cornelius Vijn on 12

152

June, but Cetshwayo's evasive reply had not reached Chelmsford. On the 28th they appeared at Mtonjaneni with another letter from Cetshwayo, together with a hundred of the captured oxen, two elephant tusks and a promise that the guns were on the way from Ulundi. The tusks were intended as a demonstration of good faith, but Chelmsford refused to accept them, saying that, as his terms had not been fully met, he would continue his advance. He agreed to delay his crossing of the White Umfolozi for another day, but he would then expect the surrender of the Zulu regiment. The 29th was used to construct a large wagon laager at Mtonjaneni in which all the tents and the bulk of the supplies were left. Two companies of the reformed 1/24th were left behind as its guards, and on the next day the whole force advanced to the south bank of the White Umfolozi, carrying rations for ten days and only one blanket, waterproof sheet and greatcoat per man.

Cetshwayo was dismayed at Chelmsford's rejection of his gifts and, with the advancing redcoats now visible from Ulundi, was becoming increasingly desperate to know how to stave off the threat to his kraal. He well knew that no regiment was likely to obey his order to surrender with their enemies in view. He sent back the envoys to say that the captured guns would be delivered the following day, and as an additional gesture he returned the Prince Imperial's sword and a hundred white oxen from his own herd. Whether Chelmsford would have responded to Cetshwayo's genuine desire to come to an agreement, as evinced by the gift of oxen, was never put to the test, for the umCijo regiment guarding the northern approaches to the river would not let them pass. Furthermore Cetshwayo's cause was not advanced by Vijn, who scribbled a note to Chelmsford saying he thought the King wanted to fight. Nevertheless Chelmsford told the envoys he would accept a thousand rifles in lieu of a regiment's surrender, and that he would not cross the Umfolozi until noon on the 3rd,

so as to give Cetshwayo time to comply. Unfortunately these concessions were never made known to the King, for when the envoys returned they were told that he had already left the royal kraal, taking Vijn with him.

On 2 July the whole of the Second Division and Flying Column were concentrated on the south bank of the White Umfolozi opposite two drifts, each 80 yards across and 700 yards apart. A stone redoubt was built to command the crossing place and some way behind it the wagons were put into laager, surrounded by an entrenchment; between the two, another laager was made to hold the draught oxen. Responsibility for the redoubt was allotted to part of No. 5 Company, Royal Engineers, and for the laagers to the remaining five companies of the 1/24th. This caused them great disappointment, for although three companies had been detached on the lines of communication, the remainder had hoped to be in at the death to avenge their comrades at Isandhlwana. The men of the new battalion, however, were little more than recruits, and Chelmsford was unwilling to risk further casualties to this regiment.

On the same day, Chelmsford received Wolseley's irate telegram of 30 June, ordering him to undertake no serious operations. He was as determined to see the business through to the end as Wolseley was to prevent him doing so, and since only 5 miles stood between him and Ulundi he had no intention of holding back now. Even if he kept his word to Cetshwayo not to advance before noon on the 3rd, Wolseley could not cover the 180 miles from Pietermaritzburg in time to stop him. (He was not to know that by then Wolseley was tossing miserably in the surf off Port Durnford.) He therefore merely acknowledged the signal.

Having received no further communication from Cetshwayo by noon of the next day, he assumed that the king intended to fight. As an indication that negotiations were at an end, he ordered the cattle which had been returned on the 28th to be driven back across the river. At

British infantry halted in sight of Ulundi. Note the cased Colours in the centre of the battalion.

1.30 p.m. he sent Buller out to reconnoitre the ground beyond the river to find a position from which he could give battle on the 4th. The track from the two drifts to Ulundi ran roughly north-east across an open expanse of grassland known as the Mahlabatini plain, passing between three large military kraals, Bulawayo, Ndabakoambe and uNodwengu, before crossing the Mbilane stream, beyond which the royal kraal stood on the lower slopes of the surrounding hills. Buller sent Baker's Horse across the upper drift where, after surprising and dispersing the Zulus on the far bank, they took up positions on a bluff to cover the subsequent withdrawal. Buller himself led the Frontier and Natal Light Horse, the Transvaal Rangers, the Edendale troop and some of the Mounted Infantry across the lower drift and headed across the plain, skirting the kraals. As they approached the Mbilane stream, they saw a party of Zulus herding some goats towards a hollow. The troopers spurred forward to round them up but Buller, suddenly suspecting a trap, bellowed at them to halt and to be prepared to open fire from the saddle. His tactical insight was well founded, for at that moment 3,000 Zulus rose from the long grass, fired a fusillade and rushed forward. Three troopers were shot dead and Buller ordered his men to retire. As they turned their horses, Captain Lord William Beresford, who had given up his post as A.D.C. to the Viceroy of India to come out to Zululand, saw that Sergeant Fitzmaurice, a big heavy man of the 24th Mounted Infantry, had fallen wounded from his horse in the path of the oncoming Zulus. He galloped back to save him, being joined by Sergeant O'Toole of the Frontier Light Horse. Together they held off the Zulus, at the same time struggling to heave the dazed Fitzmaurice on to Beresford's horse. Not without difficulty, and at great risk to their own lives, they eventually got him away. Captain D'Arcy, who had been recommended for the V.C. at Hlobane, attempted a similar rescue of Trooper Raubenheim, but as he endeavoured to hoist the wounded man on to his own horse he strained his back so badly that he was forced to drop him and only just managed to escape the assegais, riding away in acute pain. D'Arcy was subsequently awarded the Victoria Cross he had earlier been denied, as was Beresford, though the latter refused to accept it unless O'Toole was honoured as well.

As Buller's men approached the river, Baker's Horse opened fire to cover their crossing. When all were safely across, they too

The Band of the 1/13th Light Infantry.

155

Part of the British camp on the south bank of the White Umfolozi the day before Ulundi.

withdrew, covered by the Transvaal Rangers from the far bank. The whole reconnaissance had been in grave danger, but as usual Buller's alertness and powers of leadership had brought his men through.

This adventure convinced Chelmsford that the Zulus intended to fight, and, although he had that day received Wolseley's signal of 1 July about retreating on the First Division, he replied that he would do so if necessary, but that he was going to attack the Zulus on the next day. He gave out his orders that evening, telling his officers he intended to advance at first light, prior to forming his infantry in one large square which he hoped the Zulu Army would attack. No wagon laager would be used, nor trenches dug, the better to convince the Zulus, and critics of the South African Field Force, that a British square 'could beat them fairly in the open'.

To an observer, Chelmsford's men, prior to their last encounter with the Zulus, must have presented a shabby and down-at-heel aspect, particularly those battalions like the 1/13th and 90th which had been constantly in the field since January. One of the 58th wrote home: 'Our Dover friends may run away with the idea that we are the same trim, tidy and polished up individuals they have met in Snargate Street.' Although the regulars wore their home service uniforms in the traditional colours, there the resemblance ended. Their once white helmets had been dyed brown and were now soiled and battered. The scarlet serge of their frocks was sweat-stained and faded after weeks of hard wear and exposure to sun and rain, the brass buttons tarnished, and the coloured patches on the collars – blue for the 13th and 21st, black for the 58th, yellow for the 80th, buff for the 90th and green for the 94th – must have been so grimy as to be almost indistinguishable. Their dark blue trousers, discoloured by the reddish dust, would have been ripped and patched (one sapper had covered the seat of his with scarlet cloth) and their black boots and gaiters scuffed and caked with mud. Their accoutrements,

Captain Cecil D'Arcy and Sergeant E. O'Toole of the Frontier Light Horse who both won the Victoria Cross during Buller's reconnaissance on 3 July.

Chelmsford's square at Ulundi. The 9-pounders and gun teams of N/6 Battery, Royal Artillery, are in the foreground with the 1/13th Light Infantry in line beyond. Water colour by Orlando Norie.

Major J. F. Owen, R.A., with the Gatling he fired at Ulundi. Note the ammunition limber behind.

The 17th Lancers pursuing the defeated Zulus at Ulundi. Chelmsford's square can be seen in the centre background. Water colour by Charles Fripp.

which had once been bright with pipeclay, were stained like the helmets and marked with grease through constant handling. The cavalry were perhaps in better trim, though the Lancers' blue and white must have been in sorry contrast to the regiment's spotless appearance at Leeds six months before. Evidence of hard campaigning was probably less noticeable among the colonials, more practically clad in broad-brimmed hats and brown or black corduroy, though even this material tended to fade to a streaky yellow. All in all, there was nothing of Dover or Aldershot or any other of the Army's home stations about Chelmsford's troops as they tramped down to the White Umfolozi at dawn on 4 July. In its place was a rough-and-ready serviceability, allied to a quiet confidence and determination to finish their savage enemy once and for all.

At 6 a.m. Buller led out the volunteers as the advance guard, followed by the infantry with the experienced battalions of the Flying Column leading. The regular cavalry guarded the flanks and rear. By 7.30 the column had cleared the rough ground along the river bank, and the square, or rather rectangle, was formed. The leading, shorter face was manned by the five companies of the 80th in four ranks with two Gatlings of 10/7 R.A. in the centre, two 9-pounders of N/6 on the left flank and two 7-pounders of 11/7 on the right. The left face comprised the 90th Light Infantry with four companies of the 94th and two more 7-pounders of 11/7 between the battalions. Opposite, on the right face, were the 1/13th and four companies of the 58th; the remaining two guns of 11/7 were in the centre of the 13th and two 9-pounders of N/6 between the battalions. The rear face was closed by two companies of the 94th on the left, so that the whole of the left

The war artist's view of the interior of the square at Ulundi. An Illustrated London News
engraving from a sketch by Melton Prior.

View from the camp on the White Umfolozi of the smoke from the battlefield of Ulundi and the burning kraals.

rear angle was covered by that battalion, and two companies of the 2/21st filled the gap up to the remaining 9-pounders of N/6 in the other angle, behind the rear company of the 58th. Within the square were the headquarters staff, the balance of No. 5 Company, R.E., now under Chard of Rorke's Drift fame, the 2nd N.N.C., fifty wagons and mule carts with the reserve ammunition, and some hospital wagons. The volunteers and cavalry, a troop of the King's Dragoon Guards and a squadron of the 17th Lancers, protected the front, flanks and rear. In all, the force numbered 5,317, of which 1,152 were Africans. The battalions which had their Colours with them uncased them, the band of the 1/13th struck up, and the whole cumbersome formation began its

measured advance across the plain, the flanking faces keeping station behind the 80th in front and the mounted troops firing the kraals as they passed.

At 8 a.m. the square wheeled right, mounting a low ridge where it halted, each side turning outwards. The two longer sides now faced north and south respectively while the 80th's companies faced due east towards the royal kraal, just over a mile and a half away. No Zulus in any numbers had as yet been seen, and apart from the solid block of red and blue along the ridge, and the scattered groups of mounted troops, the landscape seemed empty. Archibald Forbes, the war correspondent, had offered odds of 100–1 that there would be no battle, and perhaps Chelmsford had misgivings that

162

the encounter he had sought for so long would still elude him. Then, as the Frontier Light Horse rode across the Mbilane, the entire inGobamakhosi suddenly rose out of the grass in front of them, followed by regiment after regiment springing to their feet on either side with their shields advanced. Soon the whole Zulu Army, 20,000 strong, stood arrayed in a vast horseshoe, the bulk of them encircling the north, east and southern sides of the square, while a large reserve moved round towards the burning uNodwengu kraal, poised ready to complete the circle. Once again this great warrior race stood ranked to give battle, hammering the ground with their feet and rattling their assegais against their shields; the men who had known victory at Isandhlwana and defeat at Kambula stood beside other, younger men who had yet to suffer the volleys and shells of a modern army. The veterans knew what to expect, so their confidence cannot have been high, and the natural fears of the novices probably struggled against faith in their own strength, but as one man the great host came on, swinging forward ever closer to the silent and motionless 'living laager' of red men on their rise.

The mounted troops fired from the saddle into the close-set ranks, trying to goad them into a premature charge, and then wheeled back to gallop for safety through the gaps which the infantry opened up to let them in. The battalions had fixed bayonets and formed four ranks, the front two kneeling, while along the sides and at the angles the guns and Gatlings were ready loaded, their crews about them. As soon as the cavalry cleared their front at about nine o'clock, the guns opened fire at a range of 2,000 yards. Stung by the fire, the Zulus' pace increased and, as the range closed, the artillery changed to case-shot, joined by section volleys from the infantry and the staccato rattle of the Gatlings. Such concentrated fire blasted away the leading waves of charging warriors, breaking up their mass and checking the impetus of the onslaught. A cowhide shield offered no

protection for naked limbs, no matter how high the courage that impelled them forward, and as the black bodies tumbled over in droves their comrades took cover in the long grass from which they dashed forward in ill-concerted rushes to try to get within stabbing range. A few casualties were caused within the square by Zulu marksmen but the rifle fire and case shot still crashed out and no Zulu got within 30 yards. Seeing the attack foundering, the reserve rose to its feet from its position near uNodwengu and raced forward against the south-west angle of the square. The two 9-pounders ploughed great furrows through its centre, while the 21st and 58th on either side poured their fire into the flanks. A corporal of the 58th said afterwards that the Zulu dead fell 'as though they had been tipped out of carts'. For a moment it looked as though the speed of their onset might bring them to hand-to-hand fighting, but not a single warrior reached the bayonets.

Sensing that the Zulus had shot their bolt, Chelmsford ordered the cavalry to mount. The 17th Lancers and King's Dragoon Guards trotted out between the 94th and 21st, formed line and charged the now fleeing Zulus, spearing them with their long lances as though they were pig-sticking, while at the other end of the square Buller led out the colonials and Native Horse, followed by the 2nd N.N.C. Everywhere Cetshwayo's once proud regiments were in rout, flying from the galloping horses towards the high ground at which the guns were now firing shell. The Lancers were checked at the Mbilane where a concealed party of enemy riflemen opened fire, killing Captain Wyatt-Edgell and wounding several men, but then they were across and the pursuit continued until not a live Zulu remained on the Mahlabatini plain.

It had all taken just over half an hour. The Zulu power was broken, Chelmsford had vindicated himself, and Wolseley would have to look elsewhere for glory. It had been accomplished with a loss of ten men killed and eighty-seven wounded. Over a thousand Zulu dead were counted around the square but many others were killed in the pursuit or died later from their wounds. The infantry were marched away down to the Mbilane where the men had lunch, the piles of brass cartridge cases showing where they had stood.

The site of the square is marked to this day by a garden which encloses the graves of the British who were killed and a monument which bears the names of the one officer and nine soldiers, and also a plaque: 'In Memory of the Brave Warriors who fell here in 1879 in Defence of the Old Zulu Order'.

11
Aftermath

Having accomplished the total overthrow of the Zulus in the field, Chelmsford had no intention of subordinating himself to Wolseley during the mopping-up operations that would now be necessary to complete the pacification of Zululand. When, on the day after Ulundi, he received his first official intimation of Wolseley's appointment from the Secretary of State for War, he replied that he took his supersession as a criticism of his conduct, and that since he had now defeated the Zulus he requested permission to return home. A similar message was transmitted to Wolseley. He then broke up the laager on the White Umfolozi, sending the Second Division back to Fort Newdigate and marching with the Flying Column towards St Paul's where he anticipated meeting Wolseley with the First Division.

Wolseley reached Fort Pearson at the Lower Tugela Drift on 5 July, where he received a telegram giving him news of Ulundi. This had been handed in at Landman's Drift the evening before by Archibald Forbes, who had set out on a lone ride immediately after the battle, subsequently covering the nearly 300 miles to Pietermaritzburg in fifty hours. Wolseley arrived at Port Durnford on the 7th giving Crealock the rough edge of his ill temper for the latter's lack of progress, and at once reorganized the First Division. The string of posts back to the Lower Drift with their garrisons were placed under Clifford's command, and a

column of 1,600 troops was assembled for the advance to St Paul's. Wolseley and Chelmsford met there on the 16th and, after saying goodbye to his troops, the former commander rode on to Durban with Wood and Buller, sailing for England on the 27th.

Wolseley appreciated that the first step towards the final subjugation of Zululand was the capture of the still missing Cetshwayo of whom no trace had been found after Ulundi. To this end he formed two small columns, one under Colonel Clarke of the 57th and the other under Lieutenant-Colonel Baker Russell of the 13th Hussars, one of Wolseley's 'Ring' who, with another more junior member, Captain Lord Gifford, had recently arrived in response to their master's summons. The two columns were to quarter the country north of the White Umfolozi, hitherto untouched by British troops, sending out patrols in search of the King. In an attempt to speed matters up, Wolseley offered Cornelius Vijn £200 if he could locate Cetshwayo and persuade him to give himself up. Vijn did manage to find him, but the King refused to surrender, and since he kept permanently on the move Vijn's efforts were in vain.

Wolseley established his headquarters at Ulundi and on 10 August the hunt began. Patrols rode out endlessly in all directions, searching the kraals, questioning the inhabitants, following up snippets of information and scouring every possible hiding place. Lord Gifford in particular was tireless in the quest, never sparing himself, his men or his horses; but everywhere the searchers found false trails and a wall of silence. With his movements and whereabouts always concealed owing to the loyalty of his people and their refusal, even under duress, to betray him, Cetshwayo managed to keep one jump ahead of his pursuers.

On the 26th Colonel Clarke, patrolling with the 3/60th, picked up a rumour that the King was in the remote Ngome forest, north of the Black Umfolozi. He reported to Wolseley, who sent out a strong patrol under Major Marter, K.D.G., with a squadron of that regiment, Lonsdale's Mounted Rifles, ten Mounted Infantry and a company of N.N.C. Marter's interpreter, Martin Oftebro, the son of a missionary who had been friends with Cetshwayo, acquired a clue to the King's hiding place from an oblique remark made by a Zulu in conversation. Pushing on, Marter encountered one of Gifford's runners bearing a message which disclosed that Gifford was closing in on the King but which omitted to say where. Gifford, meanwhile, had tricked a Zulu boy into leading him to the kraal where the King rested, but, after reconnoitring its location in a steep-sided clearing, he decided that his best chance of capturing Cetshwayo lay in approaching the place after dark. He had therefore moved away from the vicinity to avoid alerting the King's guardians.

A few hours after Gifford had left the area, Marter reached another kraal not far off, where Oftebro managed to discover the site of the King's kraal. Having scouted the terrain,

British officers with Zulus.

166

Cetshwayo and his wives arriving at Wolseley's camp near Ulundi escorted by officers of the King's Dragoon Guards and the 3/60th Rifles. An engraving from the Graphic.

Marter sent the N.N.C. in a circular route to block the exits from the clearing, while he led his horsemen down a steep track hidden from the kraal. At about 3 p.m. Marter charged into the clearing and surrounded the huts. Complete surprise was achieved and the Zulus offered no resistance. After being assured by Oftebro that no harm would come to him, Cetshwayo emerged from his hut to give himself up.

Two days later Marter's patrol with his royal prisoner reached Ulundi, having encountered the disappointed Gifford who rode on ahead to report the King's capture. Wolseley received Cetshwayo with due ceremony, but told him that he was to be deposed for breaking the pledges he had made at his coronation, that Zululand would be partitioned and that he would be held a prisoner. On the same day he was despatched under escort to Port Durnford for embarkation to Cape Town, where he was to be detained at the Queen's pleasure. So, sixty-three years after Shaka first founded the Zulu nation, its fourth king passed into captivity, after a war he had never sought, and in which thousands of his people had died, their kraals had been burned and their cattle seized.

With Cetshwayo a prisoner, the war was now over, barring a few minor incidents with the independently-minded tribes of the north. The final skirmish took place on the Intombi River on 8 September, where the last British casualties were incurred by the 2/4th King's Own, which, though it had been in Natal since the beginning of the war, had seen none of the major fighting. A week before, Wolseley had informed an assembly of 200 chiefs that the country was to be partitioned into thirteen kingdoms under rulers selected by him, one of which was John Dunn. Each was to keep to his own territory; the old Zulu military system with its embargoes on the marriage of younger men was to be abolished; a fair judicial process was to be established; and the sovereignty of each ruler was to be subject to supervision by a British Resident.

Wolseley's plan was essentially a short-term solution to the problem of Zululand, designed purely to ensure that the country could no longer threaten Natal or the Transvaal, without the expense of actually annexing and administering it as British territory. It took no account of Zulu sensibilities, it ignored the 1878 Boundary Commission's findings, and his choice of rulers was tactless and unwise. Within a year its defects were manifest, with constant bickering and discontent within and between the different kingdoms. By 1881 it was clear that Wolseley's settlement was a failure, but by then the British authorities were fully committed in the Transvaal where the Boers had risen in revolt. Moves to restore Cetshwayo to his kingdom were afoot, which culminated in the decision to allow him to go to England, make his peace with the Queen and discuss the future of Zululand with the Colonial Office.

In 1882, when Wolseley was at last winning the fame he longed for by quelling Arabi Pasha's revolt in Egypt, Cetshwayo arrived in London. He achieved a great popular success, both with the Queen and the British public, and received the Government's permission to resume his sovereignty over his people, subject to certain conditions and safeguards. When he eventually returned to Zululand in January 1883, however, the reality of what he found proved to be considerably less than he had anticipated. His power was diminished, his authority was questioned by many chiefs and his kingdom was reduced in size. The chief threat to his rule soon proved to be his cousin, Usibebu, who had commanded the uDhloko at Isandhlwana, had ruled one of the thirteen kingdoms, and had since been granted a territory of his own outside Cetshwayo's

Left: Usibebu, Cetshwayo's cousin, who commanded the uDhloko at Isandhlwana and opposed Cetshwayo on his return to Zululand in 1883.

jurisdiction, which unfortunately contained large numbers of the pro-Cetshwayo uSuthu faction. Unrest among the latter compelled Usibebu to repress them, trouble which escalated into ever-widening violence and fighting within Cetshwayo's territory, with Usibebu gaining the upper hand as Cetshwayo's authority crumbled. The King's troubles ended abruptly when he suddenly died on 8 February 1884, aged about sixty. The cause of death was pronounced to be heart disease, but the British medical officer who examined him suspected that he had been poisoned.

He was succeeded by his son Dinizulu to whom, a few months later, the Transvaal Boers, now independent, offered aid to overcome the increasingly powerful Usibebu. The Boers' offer was accepted, but after Usibebu had been routed Dinizulu found there was a heavy price to pay for their help. Boer demands for extensive land grants were followed by an influx of settlers pouring into Zululand, until only the territory north of the Black Umfolozi could be regarded by Dinizulu as wholly his own. Even here he was blocked off from the sea, since German traders had seized the coastal strip of St Lucia Bay.

In 1886 Dinizulu appealed to the British for help. The Germans were removed from St Lucia Bay, and eventually the Boers were induced to abide within a new boundary fixed by British and Boer negotiators. It was clear, however, that the attenuated remains of Shaka's great empire could no longer survive as an independent native state, and in 1887 Zululand was taken over as a British protectorate with Dinizulu formally recognized as Paramount Chief of the Zulus. Two years later he rebelled against British authority and was exiled, together with Tshingwayo, the victor of Isandhlwana. In 1897 Zululand was annexed to Natal. Thus, nearly twenty years after the war, Cetshwayo's kingdom became part of the colony to which it was once thought to pose such a threat.

There can be little doubt that the threat loomed larger in Sir Bartle Frere's imagination than in reality, and that his machinations to justify a pre-emptive strike against Cetshwayo were underhand and unjust. On the other hand, it must be remembered that Frere's decisions were coloured by his memories of the bloodshed and horror inflicted on Europeans when they were caught unawares by the Sepoy Mutiny in India. With such experience he may have sincerely felt that to strike first at the Zulus, warlike and bloodthirsty as they undoubtedly were, was preferable, however unjust, to the alternative (as he saw it) of waiting until the Zulus came rampaging down through an indefensible Natal. Moreover, though there is no reason to doubt, as Frere did, that Cetshwayo was equally sincere in his desire to maintain peace, it seems certain that he would never have willingly abandoned his independent status for the benefits that the then British policy of confederation might have brought to his people. Nor is there evidence that, despite the shortcomings, by European standards, of his regime, his people had any wish to change his rule for a European administration. It also seems doubtful whether, given the pent-up frustration built into the Zulu military system, Cetshwayo would have been able to restrain his warriors much longer from fighting, either within or outside Zululand, no matter what his own preferences were. The conflicting pressures between the different factions and territories in South Africa at the time made an explosion inevitable sooner or later, as indeed occurred between Briton and Boer in 1881 and again in 1899.

If Frere had not taken action against the Zulus, and if his worst fears of rampant Zulu militarism sparking off black uprisings all over southern Africa had been realized, the ensuing slaughter would have been far greater than that incurred in the Zulu War. It seems unlikely that, for prestige, strategic and economic reasons, the British Empire would have allowed such a rebellion to go unpunished. On the other hand, opposition to Imperialism in Britain, which in fact contributed to the return of a Liberal government after the Zulu War, might, in the event of a more widespread holocaust, have demanded a retreat from south-east Africa. If it had, the vacuum left by Britain would inevitably have been filled either by the Boers or by another European power. Germany in 1880 was more concerned with consolidating her position in Europe than acquiring colonies, but she was developing links with the Boer republics, she was to claim territory in east and south-west Africa in 1884 and the incursion at St Lucia Bay in the same year was a foretaste of interest in south-east Africa. Had she been able to become the dominant European power in that area in the closing decades of the nineteenth century, the events of the twentieth would have been changed indeed for black and white alike.

Such possibilities are, of course, pure speculation. Nevertheless, in the climate of those times, with more and more of Africa being partitioned off between the European powers, an independent native kingdom like Zululand could not have retained its sovereignty for long, even if Frere had held his hand in 1879. Although neither Frere's invasion nor Wolseley's settlement improved the lot of the Zulus, their destiny under another colonial power might have been far worse, like the later genocidal repression of the Hereros in German South-West Africa. If the Zulu War, however unjust it might have been, indirectly spared them that fate, the dead of both sides did not die in vain.

Left and Above: The South African campaign medal with clasp for the Zulu War. This particular medal belonged to Major R. J. C. Marter, King's Dragoon Guards, who captured Cetshwayo.

Appendix A

British Regiments and Corps of the Zulu War and Subsequent Designations

1st King's Dragoon Guards; 1st The Queen's Dragoon Guards (1959).

17th Lancers; 17th/21st Lancers (1922).

Royal Artillery.

Royal Engineers.

3rd (East Kent) Regiment (Buffs); Buffs (Royal East Kent) (1881); Queens's (1966).

4th (King's Own) Regiment; King's Own Royal Lancaster (1881); King's Own Royal Border (1959).

13th (Somersetshire) Light Infantry; Somerset Light Infantry (1881); Light Infantry (1968).

21st Royal Scots Fusiliers; Royal Scots Fusiliers (1881); Royal Highland Fusiliers (1959).

24th (2nd Warwickshire) Regiment; South Wales Borderers (1881); Royal Regiment of Wales (1969).

57th (West Middlesex) Regiment; 1st Middlesex (1881); Queen's (1966).

58th (Rutlandshire) Regiment; 2nd Northamptonshire (1881); Royal Anglian (1964).

60th King's Royal Rifle Corps; King's Royal Rifle Corps (1881); Royal Green Jackets (1966).

80th (Staffordshire Volunteers) Regiment; 2nd South Staffordshire (1881); Staffordshire (1959).

88th (Connaught Rangers) Regiment; 1st Connaught Rangers; disbanded 1922.

90th (Perthshire Volunteers) Light Infantry; 2nd Cameronians (1881); disbanded 1968.

91st (Argyllshire) Highlanders; 1st Argyll and Sutherland Highlanders (1881).

94th Regiment; 2nd Connaught Rangers; disbanded 1922.

99th (Duke of Edinburgh's) Regiment; 2nd Wiltshire (1881); Duke of Edinburgh's Royal (1959).

Commissariat & Transport Department; | Army Service Corps (1888); Royal Corps of
Army Service Corps; | Transport (1965).

Army Hospital Staff; |
Army Hospital Corps; | Royal Army Medical Corps (1898).

Ordnance Store Branch and Corps; Royal Army Ordnance Corps (1922).

Appendix B

Zulu Corps and Regiments in 1879

Corps	Regiment	Raised by	Age	Numbers
uSixepi	Same	Shaka	80	Negligible
	Nokenke	Mpande	30	2,000
umBelebele	Same	Shaka	78	Negligible
	umHlanga	Mpande	28	1,000
uMhlambongwenya	Same	Shaka	75	Negligible
	umXapo	Mpande	35	1,000
uDukuza	Same	Shaka	73	Negligible
	Iqwa	Mpande	35	500
Bulawayo	Same	Shaka	70	Negligible
	Nsugamgeni	Mpande	35	1,000
uDlambedhlu	Same	Dingane	68	Negligible
	Ngwekwe	Mpande	55	1,000
	Ngulubi	Mpande	55	500
Nodwengu	umKhlulutshane	Dingane	64	Negligible
	umSikaba	Mpande	54	500
	uDududu	Mpande	35	1,500
	Mbubi	Mpande	35	500
	Isanqu	Mpande	54	1,500
Undi	uThulwane	Mpande	45	1,500
	Nkonkone	Mpande	43	500
	Ndhlondhlo	Mpande	43	900
	inDlu-yengwe	Mpande	28	1,000
	inGobamakhosi	Cetshwayo	24	6,000

Corps	Regiment	Raised by	Age	Numbers
uDhloko	Same	Mpande	40	2,500
	amaKwenke	Mpande	29	1,500
umCijo	Same	Mpande	28	2,500
	unQakamatye	Mpande	30	5,000
	uMtulisazwi	Mpande	29	1,500
uVe	Same	Cetshwayo	23	3,500
	uMzinyati	Mpande	43	500
umBonambi	Same	Mpande	32	1,500
	Amashutu	Mpande	32	500

(From a list compiled by Ian J. Knight for the Victorian Military Society's Zulu War Centenary Publication.)

Bibliography

Chadwick, G. A., *The Battle of Isandhlwana and the Defence of Rorke's Drift*, Natal Educational Association, Natal, n.d.

Coupland, Reginald, *Zulu Battle Piece – Isandhlwana*, Collins, London, 1948.

Emery, Frank, *The Red Soldier*, Hodder & Stoughton, London, 1977.

Featherstone, Donald, *Captain Carey's Blunder*, Leo Cooper, London, 1973.

Featherstone, Donald, *Weapons and Equipment of the Victorian Soldier*, Blandford Press, Poole, 1978.

Field Exercises and Evolutions of Infantry, 1870 and 1877, H.M.S.O.

Furneaux, Rupert, *The Zulu War*, Weidenfeld & Nicolson, London, 1963.

Glover, Michael, *Rorke's Drift*, Leo Cooper, London, 1975.

The Graphic, 1879.

The Illustrated London News, 1879.

Jackson, F. W. D., 'Isandhlwana – The Sources Re-examined', *Journal of the Society for Army Historical Research (J.S.A.H.R.)*, Volume XLIII, 1965.

Langley, D. E. and Knight, I. J. (ed.), *There will be an Awful Row at Home about This*, Victorian Military Society Zulu War Centenary Publication, 1979.

Lloyd, Alan, *The Zulu War*, Hart-Davis MacGibbon, London, 1973.

Morris, Donald R., *The Washing of the Spears*, Jonathan Cape, London, 1966.

Parry, D. H., *Britain's Roll of Glory*, Cassell, London, 1895.

Regulations for the Field Forces in South Africa, 1878 and 1879, H.M.S.O.

Selby, John, *Shaka's Heirs*, Allen and Unwin, London, 1971.

South African Military Historical Society Journal, Volume 4, Numbers 4 and 5, Zulu War Centenary Issues, 1979.

Tylden, Major G., 'Commandant George Hamilton-Browne', *J.S.A.H.R.*, Volume XXXVII, 1959.

Tylden, Major G., 'Inhlobane Mountain and Kambula', *J.S.A.H.R.*, Volume XXXI, 1953.

Tylden, Major G., 'Mounted Infantry', *J.S.A.H.R.*, Volume XXII, 1944.

Tylden, Major G., 'Some Aspects of the Zulu War', *J.S.A.H.R.*, Volume XVII, 1938.

Tylden, Major G., 'The Frontier Light Horse', *J.S.A.H.R.*, Volume XVIII, 1939.

Wilkinson-Latham, Robert, *Uniforms and Weapons of the Zulu War*, Batsford, London, 1978.

Wolseley, Viscount, *The Soldier's Pocket Book*, Macmillan, London, 1886.

Wood, Sir Evelyn, *British Battles by Land and Sea*, Cassell, London, 1915.

Wood, Sir Evelyn, *From Midshipman to Field Marshal*, Volume II, Methuen, London, 1906.

Various Regimental Histories and Journals.

Index

Figures in italic refer to page numbers of illustrations.

179